THE ROD, THE ROOT
AND THE FLOWER

COVENTRY PATMORE
From a sketch by J. S. Sargent, R.A. 1894

THE ROD, THE ROOT
AND THE FLOWER

by

COVENTRY PATMORE

EDITED AND WITH AN
INTRODUCTION BY
DEREK PATMORE

✣ Angelico Press

First published in 1950
by Grey Walls Press Limited, London

Second edition, Angelico Press, 2013
Foreword © Stratford Caldecott, 2013

For information, address:
Angelico Press, 4619 Slayden Rd., NE
Tacoma, WA 98422
www.angelicopress.com

ISBN 978-1-62138-036-8

Cover Design: Cristy Deming

CONTENTS

FOREWORD

WHY WE NEED
COVENTRY PATMORE

COVENTRY PATMORE (1823–1896) was an English Victorian mystical poet and essayist, very well known in his time, who fell into undeserved obscurity during the twentieth century. Privately educated, he at first wanted to become an artist, then a scientist, but instead became one of the most celebrated poets of his day.

Under the influence of Alfred Lord Tennyson, Patmore published his first small volume of *Poems* in 1844. After receiving a particularly cruel review he tried to destroy the edition, but it was too late: his career was already launched, and through this first book he soon made the acquaintance of the Pre-Raphaelite Brotherhood, especially Dante Gabriel Rossetti and William Holman Hunt, and began to move in their circles. In order to earn money while trying to write he became an assistant librarian in the British Museum.

Patmore was happily married three times in succession, and his best poetry is associated with and inspired by the theme of marriage. In fact, he could be called the Poet of the Theology of the Body. His most famous poem, *The Angel in the House*, was written between 1854 and 1862, at which point he lost his first wife, Emily, who had given him six children. During the following three years he drew ever closer to the Catholic Church, and while on a visit to Rome fell in love with a devout Catholic, whom he thought was the poor companion of a wealthy woman. When he discovered that she was in fact *herself* the wealthy woman, he ran away in panic at the thought of becoming a kept man, but was brought back by friends, and he and Mary were married following his own reception into the Church by Cardinal Manning.

The English Reformation cast a long shadow, and despite Catholic Emancipation in the early 19th century and the influence of distinguished English converts such as Manning himself and Blessed John Henry Newman, to become a Papist in nineteenth century England was still something of a disgrace, so that Patmore's reputation was adversely affected by his reception into the Catholic Church. John Ruskin, who had at first admired him, thought that by becoming "sectarian" (as he saw it) "all his fine thinking" had been rendered "ineffectual to us English."

In 1877 Patmore published what everyone now regards as his best work, *The Unknown Eros* (encouraged by his saintly daughter, Mary Christina, who became a nun), and in the following year *Amelia*, his own favorite among his poems, with an interesting and influential essay on *English Metrical Law* as a kind of preface to it. As he himself pointed out years later, the basic principles of this essay became widely accepted among critics within a decade or two.

In 1880 his second wife died, and he married only a year later, at the age of 58, the woman who had been the governess of his children. Patmore was of course by then a friend or acquaintance of many of the literary figures in Victorian England, including Tennyson, Carlisle, and Browning. He became particular friends with Alice Meynell (with whom he fell in love), Francis Thompson (rescued from the streets by the Meynells and soon to be a close friend and disciple), Robert Bridges, and Gerard Manley Hopkins, whom he met in 1883 and who was the one who first drew Bridges to his attention. Bridges in turn wanted to enlist Patmore's support for his and Hopkins's experiments in accentual verse, which he claimed amounted to a "new prosody." Patmore, however, did not fully understand or appreciate Hopkins's poems (perhaps he was too old at this point), commenting that they were like "veins of pure gold imbedded in masses of impracticable quartz."

For his part, Hopkins wrote detailed criticisms of many of Patmore's poems, protesting at "moral blasphemies" in them and a "passion for paradox" that occasionally tortured his sensibility, though he admired Patmore's mastery of the English language. Patmore respected his friend's critical judgment enough to burn in

1887 a series of his poems that Hopkins did not like, called *Sponsa Dei*. (It should be noted that Hopkins was mortified to hear that he had done so.)

What had shocked Hopkins was the intensity of the sexual-mystical symbolism of the poems. However, the insights expressed in these suppressed poems were not completely lost. You can find them scattered through Patmore's last two books of essays and aphorisms, *Religio Poetae* in 1893, and my own favorite of his works, published two years later, *The Rod, the Root and the Flower*, which Herbert Read compared to Pascal's *Pensées*. This was published in 1896, the year before Patmore died.

Beyond Romanticism

Patmore was a Romantic in many ways—not least because the main theme of his writing was "romance" or love, especially the love between husband and wife. He was one of those eminent Victorians who inherited and transformed the legacy of the Romantic Movement, but it is not fair to call him, simply, a "Romantic." He was much more balanced, and more interesting, than that.

The era of European civilization marked by the French Revolution was torn between Rationalism and Romanticism. If Rationalism glorified the idea of universal order attained through the use of Reason, Romanticism was a rejection of intellectual order in the name of self-expression: it is associated in philosophy above all with "the turn to the subject" (influenced perhaps by German Pietism about "me and God") and away from objectivism in philosophy. The question of "the" truth was swept away, leaving rather a concern with what was true *for me* and *for you* (hence historicism, evolutionism, relativism, and irony)—a glorification of the "active, dynamic and imaginative self," the attempt to "express" the world rather than "describe" it. And thus nature herself becomes a form of self-expression (Hegel), and therefore "symbolic" (Schelling, then Coleridge). The finite expresses or at least *gestures towards* the infinite, and everything that exists is full of meaning—meanings too rich or elusive to be adequately captured in prose, or even poetry. Romanticism therefore in its secular and literary form tends towards a nostalgia for religious belief, and substitutes for the religious quest for God a quest for the infinite Self—perhaps (as became more manifest in the twentieth century) in the depths of the Unconscious, which was itself an invention or discovery of the Romantics (Schelling, well before Freud or Jung).

Thus in Britain we find the Rationalism of the Royal Society and the Scottish Enlightenment philosophers—a cult of "universal Reason"—and the Industrial Revolution based on that Rationalism, opposed by poets such as William Blake, Samuel Taylor Coleridge, and William Wordsworth in the name of the "creative imagination." Another important strand in English Romanticism was a tendency to glorify the art and architecture of the Middle Ages, which led to a revival of Gothic architecture, encouraged by the Christian Socialist John Ruskin. Out of this Romantic stream of influence grew in the second half of the century the Pre-Raphaelite Brotherhood (also fostered by Ruskin), with their rebellion against Victorian morality, and the Arts and Crafts movement led by William Morris. The Pre-Raphaelites (Dante Gabriel Rossetti, Edward Burne-Jones, Edward Millais, and later Morris) sought to challenge the modernism (i.e., Raphaelitism) of art in their day by a return to medieval sources, to nature, tradition, and allegory— Chesterton later described Ruskin as wanting every part of the medieval cathedral except the altar. They found some of their inspiration in the Arthurian romances and the novels of Sir Walter Scott. Finally there was the Aesthetic Movement of G.F. Watts, James Whistler, and Walter Pater—a cult of "art for art's sake," often coupled with sexual license, perhaps best represented by the dissolute Oscar Wilde, who ended his life as a repentant Catholic. To Pater, the purpose of life was to burn always with a "hard, gemlike flame," to live in continual aesthetic ecstasy. The painters in the group were interested in shapes and colors, in art as decoration rather than the imitation or understanding of nature.

In between Romanticism and the Rationalist movement it opposed, the Catholic Literary Revival separated itself from both as they turned increasingly against Christianity and traditional morality. Thus the Catholic Revival could be described as a Christian *literature of protest* not just against the mechanization of life, scientific positivism, and the bourgeois mentality of Victorian England, but also against liberalism and relativism in religion. While it had many of its roots in Romanticism, it was, as Chesterton noted in *The Victorian Age in Literature*, "a rational movement; almost a rationalist movement." It was a "protest of the rationality of religion as against the increasing irrationality of mere Victorian comfort and compromise." Thus it transcended the dichotomy of the age. In 1845, when Newman converted to Roman Catholicism at Littlemore, he had already seen that the real choice was not between Reason and Emotion, as most Victorians still thought, but between the Mechanical and the Supernatural order—or between a conception of life based on industry and technology on the one hand, and a conception of life based upon religion on the other. And it was already apparent to Newman that the Catholic Church was the only institution that could be trusted to defend human Reason, human Feeling, and the Supernatural—all three at the same time and in harmony.

Romantic artists and poets tended to elevate feeling above intellect, poetry above philosophy, and nature above man or God, and in so doing lost their balance and eventually their hold on reality. The Christian Romantics of the Literary Revival, by contrast, were intellectuals in search of the truth. They wanted the *whole* of reality, which could not be grasped simply through feeling, any more than it could be grasped by rational thought on its own. You might put it this way. In traditional Scholastic philosophy, Being is characterized by unity, truth, goodness, and beauty. The Romantics tended to subsume truth and goodness within beauty, believing that beauty alone could take them to their goal. Christian Romantics knew that beauty on its own could easily lead us astray. Beauty, Truth, and Goodness "coinhere," they belong together, and if you separate them they will wither and die.

These writers wanted truth. That is, they wanted the Logos. They were not merely indulging themselves and exploring their own feeling. Through *poetry*, through *images*, through *music*, through *beauty*, and through *story* they sought to reveal the presence of an invisible (but objective) spiritual world underlying the visible. The current popularity of fantasy writing is partly their legacy—especially that of Lewis and Tolkien. They awoke in our culture a hunger for the meaning and truth that are to be found in history, in drama, in heroism—living images that reveal glimpses of a higher reality, a spiritual reality that walks among us in the light of day. They awoke a renewed appreciation of the importance of *symbols* as a vehicle of metaphysical and doctrinal truth. And for this reason, in the following century they became entwined and associated with the *nouvelle théologie* and the *ressourcement* that took Catholic thinkers back to the patristic era, to the "sacramental imagination" of the early Fathers, and a renewed appreciation of the spiritual and allegorical interpretation of Scripture.

The Sixth Day

All of this is reflected in Coventry Patmore. His milieu was at the heart of the Catholic Literary Revival, and his insights fit perfectly with those of the *nouvelle théologie* that came later. "Nature fulfilled by grace is not less natural, but is supernaturally natural,"[†] captures the paradoxical truth at the core of Henri de Lubac's interpretation of St Thomas. In the first chapter of *Religio Poetae* Patmore develops a distinction akin to that which Newman drew between *intellectual assent* to truths of faith, and their *apprehension* or *comprehension* as a matter of actual perception, which is the experience of the poets, and especially of the saints. He writes prophetically:

> I do not see what is to become of popular Religion, parodied and discredited as Christianity is by the 'religions' of Atheists, Moralists, Formalists, Philanthropists, Scientists, and Sentimentalists, unless there can be infused into it some increased longing and capacity for real apprehension.

The reason poets, he adds, are so important, is that "the Poet is, *par excellence*, the *perceiver*, nothing having any interest for him, unless he can, as it were, see and touch it with the spiritual senses, with which he is preeminently endowed." The Saints may also have these spiritual senses "greatly developed by their holiness and their habitual suppression of the corporeal senses," but they necessarily tend to express themselves with greater

† *The Rod, the Root, and the Flower*, p. 28.

circumspection. The Poet can speak what others cannot, because he occupies a position "somewhere between that of a Saint and that of Balaam's Ass." His gift is to be able to detect, "in external nature, those likenesses and echoes by which spiritual realities can alone be rendered credible and more or less apparent, or subject to 'real apprehension' in persons of inferior perceptive powers." So the Poet is able to bring these spiritual realities within the grasp of others.

Christianity, he concludes in this first essay, is "yet in its infancy, though it seems, as it has always seemed to contemporaries, to be in its decay." He even looks forward to something like a "New Dispensation" of Christianity in which the "real apprehension" of the truths of faith will be opened to the millions. Many of these truths concern the relation between man and woman, and here he anticipates in many respects the Theology of the Body of Pope John Paul II—a theology grounded in the Trinity, and based on the analogies between the love of the soul for God, the love of God for mankind, and the love between man and woman. His formulations can be startling. He writes, for example: "The account of the creation, in Genesis, is prophecy, not history. We are now in the beginning of the sixth day. Woman is being created out of man."[†]

For woman, as he says, "is the sum and complex of all

† Ibid., p. 48.

nature, and is the *visible* glory of God. The divine manhood, indeed, may be *discerned* in man through the cloud of that womanhood of which he is a participator, inasmuch as he also is the Body, which, as St Augustine says, 'is the Bride.'"† Creation, he says, is a musical concert, "consisting of representative repetitions and variations upon the single theme, God, who is defined by St Thomas as an *Act*—the Act of love, the 'embrace' of the First and Second Persons, and their unity is the thence proceeding Spirit of Life, 'Creator Spiritus,' the Life and Joy of all things." To hear it we must fix our attention

> upon the *theme*, which is God, and '*the love which is between Himself*,' the love of which all other loves are more or less remote echoes and refrains. This 'dry doctrine' of the Trinity, or primary Act of Love, is the keynote of all living knowledge and delight. God himself becomes a concrete object and an intelligible joy when contemplated as the eternal felicity of a Lover with the beloved, the Anti-type and very original of the Love which inspires the Poet and the thrush.‡

Patmore even saw why the time had come for the Church to unfold a Theology of the Body. "It is because religion is less venerated now than ever, and love more, that it has become permissible to look a little behind the veils which have hitherto concealed these truths from the many, though they have always shone clearly to

---

† Ibid., p.113.
‡ Ibid., p.111.

God's Elect, to whom 'Thy Maker is thy Husband' is no
hyperbole or figure of speech."†

It is not surprising, therefore, to find reflected in Patmore's poetry and other writings a great love for the
Blessed Virgin Mary.

> Thou Speaker of all wisdom in a Word,
> Thy Lord!
> Speaker who thus could'st well afford
> Thence to be silent;—ah, what silence that
> Which had for prologue thy "Magnificat?"—
> O, Silence full of wonders
> More than by Moses in the Mount were heard,
> More than were utter'd by the Seven Thunders;
> Silence that crowns, unnoted, like the voiceless blue,
> The loud world's varying view,
> And in its holy heart the sense of all things ponders!

These verses are from the splendid poem "The Child's
Purchase" from *The Unknown Eros*, which contains an
entire Mariology. A bit later in the same section, we
read:

> My Lady, yea, the Lady of my Lord,
> Who didst the first descry
> The burning secret of virginity,
> We know with what reward!
> Prism whereby
> Alone we see
> Heav'n's light in its triplicity;
> Rainbow complex

† Ibid., pp. 113–114.

In bright distinction of all beams of sex,
Shining for aye
In the simultaneous sky,
To One, thy Husband, Father, Son, and Brother,
Spouse blissful, Daughter, Sister, milk-sweet Mother;
Ora pro me!

Indeed, this is the sixth day, and in the Blessed Virgin woman is created, and from her are born all who now live. The great secret, Patmore says, that the Church has hidden in plain sight of all, as the Sun is hidden by its rays, is "the doctrine of the Incarnation, regarded not as an historical event which occurred two thousand years ago, but as an event which is renewed in the body of every one who is in the way to the fulfillment of his original destiny."[†] Our Lady is the "prism" or "rainbow" in whom we can see this dazzling secret that reveals our destiny.

It seems to me that in Patmore's poetry, essays, and aphorisms, we see a fullness of Catholic wisdom that is not exceeded by any other representative of the Revival, and one that speaks to our age as much as it does to his own, opening vistas within the Word of God that remain incompletely explored even today.

STRATFORD CALDECOTT

---

† Ibid., p.124.

INTRODUCTION

By DEREK PATMORE

COVENTRY PATMORE published this book a year before his death in 1896. It was the final flowering of his talent. In this last work he summed up his very personal philosophy about human and divine love. *The Rod, The Root, and the Flower* represents the results of those years of meditation during which the poet had practically withdrawn from any form of social or public life. It is the least known of Patmore's works. The original edition was small, and, being a work in prose—and difficult prose—it appealed to a very limited public. Yet I venture to think that it remains amongst his most important works, and that is one of the reasons why I have prepared this new edition of a book which has been practically unobtainable for many years.

Frederick Page, one of the most discerning of Patmore's critics, has written: 'His theory of sex is part of his theology. This is what the writers of handbooks say, but they look abroad into mystical experiences not their own; Patmore looked into human marriage.' It is this interpretation of love from his own personal experience which makes Patmore's writings so unusual and often challenging to the modern mind. This Victorian poet and mystic had faith. He believed in his mission as a poet, and he was convinced of the ennobling qualities of pure love.

These aphorisms, often veiled and sometimes bitter in their truth, are Patmore's final affirmation of his creed that 'Lovers are nothing else than Priest and Priestess to each other of the Divine Manhood and the Divine Womanhood which are in God'. Revolutionary as this idea must have sounded to many of his late Victorian readers, it had run all through his poetry, and the germ of it is even found in his popular success, *The Angel In The House*. Tradition has identified 'The Angel' with his first wife, Emily, but although this long narrative poem undoubtedly contains memories and evocations of his adored wife the poet meant the title to be symbolical. 'The Angel In The House', in the words of Frederick Page, 'is conscious love, uniting its subject and object, Man, Woman, God.'

Any reader who wants to understand and appreciate *The Rod, The Root, and theFlower* must remember that Coventry Patmore was a poet an d mystic obsessed with a special philosophy of his own. Osbert Burdett, commenting upon this, wrote in his *The Idea Of Coventry Patmore:*

> He is one of the few poets who have tried to build a philosophy out of the experiences of love;and his attempt is original because it is not, as were previous attempts, based upon any disregard or arbitrary manipulation of facts; but was inspired by an unusually frank admission of them.

But where Patmore differed from most poets was in the fact that he believed that the perfection of human love could be only found in marriage. Deeply religious by nature and a convert to the Roman Catholic Church in the middle of his life, he did not approve of illicit passions. Undoubtedly the teachings of the Catholic faith greatly helped him to develop his philosophy, and the following work confirms that he was deeply read in the writings of the great Catholic mystics. At the same time, he was also influenced by the works of Plato and some of the finest odes in *The Unknown Eros* show this influence.

To-day, we are apt to think that only modern psychologists understand the mysteries of love. But Coventry Patmore forestalled many of their conclusions during his lonely exploration into the secrets of the human heart. In *The Rod, The Root and The Flower* will be found sayings like:

> The external man and woman are each the projected simulacrum of the latent half of the other, and they do but love themselves in thus loving their opposed likenesses.

Such statements foreshadow Otto Weininger and Freud, although their authority can be traced back to Plato and to the Catholic mystical writers, but they demonstrate that the intellectuals of the Catholic faith are often more modern than non-Catholics will suppose.

Recently Patmore's writings have been attracting the attention of leading French writers, especially François Mauriac and Paul Claudel, and after reading his last works it is easy to understand why these writings should find admirers amongst Catholic intellectuals abroad. Claudel, in particular, has devoted several essays to analysing this English poet's work, and he has introduced his poetry to

French readers by translating a number of *The Unknown Eros* odes into French.

Perhaps it is natural that Coventry Patmore's works should attract attention abroad, for, by becoming a Catholic he, unlike most Victorian writers and poets, entered into the current of European thought. It is often forgotten that he studied at the Collège de France as a young man, and that he was widely read in French and German literature. He was always deeply attracted to German philosophy, especially to that of Schopenhauer. These foreign influences may account for the many un-English qualities to be found in Patmore's work, although in character he remained essentially British: no other country could have produced so contradictory and paradoxical a personality.

Claudel, who as a great Catholic writer understands Patmore's philosophy and work, states in an essay in *Positions et Propositions* that Patmore's life and work was dominated by two ideas—that of married love and that of a finished world. He explains that Patmore did not share the prevalent Victorian belief of an infinite world. He agrees with Patmore by writing:

> Le monde n'est pas infini. Il est inépuisable, ce qui est bien différent.'

Patmore forestalled Claudel's idea in his ode *Legam Tuam Dilexi:*

> The 'Infinite'. Word horrible! at feud
> With life, and the braced mood
> Of power and joy and love;
> Forbidden, by wise heathen ev'n, to be
> Spoken of Deity,

Whose Name, on popular altars, was 'The Unknown'.
Because, or ere It was reveal'd as One
Confined in Three,
The people fear'd that it prove
Infinity . . .

Coventry Patmore, like Claudel, also thought that man could only find salvation by seeking the love of God. As he wrote: 'All men are led to Heaven by their own loves.' He believed in the refining quality of human and divine love but he had no delusions about the frailties of mankind. Indeed, he was sunk in despair when he meditated upon the future of England. He warned his favourite son, nicknamed Piffie: 'Poor Piffie, you have a hard time in front of you.'

In contrast to the optimism of most of his contemporaries, he had little faith in the future of democracy. He mistrusted the intelligence of the masses, and looking ahead with a prophet's vision, he saw a state of society which closely resembles that of post-war England. In one of his political essays he wrote: 'Neither the voter nor the inspector yet know their power and opportunities: but they soon will. We shall have to "square" the district surveyor once or twice a year, lest imaginary drains become a greater terror than real typhoid; we shall have to smoke our pipes secretly and with a sense of sin, lest the moral supervisor of the parish should decline our offer of a half-crown for holding his nose during the weekly examination of our bedrooms and closets; . . . we shall have to tip our policemen and inspectors for looking over our infractions of popular moralities of a newer pattern.'

Faced with such a dismal future, he believed that mankind

could only be redeemed by things of the spirit. As he wrote: 'If society is to survive its apparently impending dangers, it must be mainly by guarding and increasing the purity of the sources in which society begins. The world is finding out, as it has often done before, that it cannot do without religion. Love is the first thing to wither under its loss. What love does in transfiguring life, that religion does in transfiguring love; as anyone may see who compares one state or time with another.'

The transfiguring power of love, both human and divine —this is the message that runs right through *The Rod, The Root, and The Flower*. Alas, it is one which finds little echo in this unhappy and distracted post-war world. But Patmore's message, although not always easy to understand at first, will bring consolation to those who still seek a solution to our present problems.

This last published prose work of Patmore's also has a special interest as it undoubtedly contains many of the ideas which he had expressed some years earlier in the lost prose work, *Sponsa Dei*. Controversy has raged round the question whether Gerard Manley Hopkins actually persuaded the older poet to destroy this book or not, but a recently discovered letter from Hopkins to Patmore, written after he had visited him at Hastings and read the manuscript, seems to confirm the fact that Hopkins's disapproval did make Patmore decide to burn it.

Sir Edmund Gosse, one of the few who read the manuscript, wrote of *Sponsa Dei:*

This vanished masterpiece was not very long, but polished

and modulated to the highest degree of perfection. No existing specimen of Patmore's prose seems so delicate, or penetrated by quite so high a charm of style as this last book was ...

The subject of it was certainly audacious. It was not more or less than an interpretation of the love between the soul and God by an analogy of the love between a woman and a man; it was, indeed, a transcendental treatise on Divine desire seen through the veil of human desire. The purity and crystalline passion of the writer carried him safely over the most astounding difficulties, but perhaps, on the whole, he was right in considering that it should not be shown to the vulgar. Yet the scruple which destroyed it was simply deplorable; the burning of *Sponsa Dei* involved a distinct loss to literature.

Coventry Patmore burnt the manuscript of *Sponsa Dei* on Christmas Day, 1887—a year and a half after he had shown it to Gerard Manley Hopkins. It was not the first time he had destroyed his own work, but it must be remembered that he had the highest regard for Hopkin's literary and religious opinions. He consulted Hopkins about the revision of his work for the collected edition of his poems, and even if the young Jesuit priest did not actually advise Patmore to destroy this prose work, there is little doubt that his disapproval weighed heavily with Patmore and helped to decide on its destruction.

Alice Meynell, however, always declared that although Patmore burnt the *Sponsa Dei*, much of its substance is still to be found in *The Rod, The Root, and The Flower*. Her opinion seems to be confirmed by a letter which Coventry Patmore wrote to a friend in 1888 where he said:

I did not burn *Sponsa Dei* altogether withal ... I talked with Dr. Rouse about it, and he seemed to have no strong opinions one way or another, but said he thought that all the substance of the work was already published in my poems and in one or two of my papers (in *St. James's Gazette*).

Lastly, Herbert Read, one of the best of Patmore's modern critics, writes commenting upon the loss of *Sponsa Dei:*

> One cannot help regretting the destruction of this work (as we regret the poems which Hopkins, for similar scruples, himself, destroyed), but actually I doubt if much of the substance of Patmore's doctrines has been lost. It is all implicit in the Odes, and in that book of maxims which is one of the greatest of Patmore's achievements, *The Rod, The Root, and The Flower* (an English work which it is not wholly ridiculous to compare with Pascal's *Pensées*).

Some people may object to the many Catholic doctrines enunciated in this book, but Patmore himself wrote in his Preface that he was addressing all Christians, whether they be Catholic or outside the visible Church. He always held very original views about religion, and although he became a devout Catholic, he reserved the right to criticise the priesthood and even, at times, murmured against the Pope.

Like the men of the Renaissance, he merged the cult of beauty with that of the Virgin Mary and he did not scruple to use pagan myths to illustrate Catholic truths. There is much of Plato's teachings in his work and this makes it provocative to the modern mind. Indeed, the manner in which Patmore used to find Catholic affinities in antique art shocked many of his contemporaries. Friends, too, like Aubrey De Vere and Gerard Manley Hopkins, recoiled before the passionate and often pagan utterances of the *Eros And Psyche* odes, and the majority of Victorian readers were disturbed by the manner in which Patmore used the Greek myth to interpret the love of the Soul for God.

It would be unjust, however, to think that this poet was obsessed only with the mysteries of love and religion. He could be very human and unexpectedly sensitive to the world around him. Coventry Patmore is too often portrayed as the arrogant and wilful mystic, yet even *The Rod, The Root, and The Flower* contains such human statements as the following:

> Every act of goodwill permanently and sensibly increases goodwill. Trifling acts of goodwill are often more efficacious in this way than great ones. A flower given in kindness and at the right time profits more, both to giver and receiver, than some vast material benefit in which the goodwill is hidden by the magnitude of the act.

Coventry Patmore also had very definite views on the poet's function. His conception of the poet's place in society was fine and noble. He compared the Poet with the Saint, and he saw him as the 'perceiver'. Describing his ideal poet he wrote of him as 'nothing having any interest for him unless he can, as it were, see it and touch it with the spiritual senses, with which he is pre-eminently endowed'. He had no patience with some of his contemporary poets who compromised with popular taste, and he once remarked that he was the only poet of his generation, except Barnes, who steadily maintained a literary conscience.

It is this intellectual integrity which makes Patmore's writings of particular interest to the reader of to-day. For this Victorian poet, who was outside the current of his period, saw beyond the boundaries of the nineteenth century and dared to affront the future. There is an edge and a crystalline brightness to many of the aphorisms in *The Rod, The Root, and the Flower* which are the result of clear thinking and of deep meditation. If this work were not dated 1895 it might have been written centuries earlier or in modern times, for in summing up his philosophy Patmore drew upon many sources. Here are echoes of Plato, of St. Theresa, of St. John of the Cross, and passages that foreshadow contemporary sex psychology. On re-reading this book, I have been reminded of a remark from André Gide's *Journals* where he says:

> All great works of art are rather difficult of access. The reader who thinks them easy has failed to penetrate to the heart of the matter. That mysterious heart has no need of obscurity to defend it against an over-bold approach; clarity does this well enough.

I venture to think that this book has something of that sort of clarity.

In editing this new edition I have used the same text as that in the original edition issued by Messrs. G. Bell & Sons, but in re-printing the Aphorisms and Extracts at the end of the book I have added a number of hitherto unpublished ones from the original manuscript now in the Library of Nottingham University, and I acknowledge with grateful thanks the permission of Nottingham University for allowing me to do so. I also thank Messrs. G. Bell & Sons for permission to use copyright material, and Messrs. Secker & Warburg for permission to quote an extract from André Gide's *Journals*.

PREFACE

By COVENTRY PATMORE

IF ST. AUGUSTINE FOUND IT necessary to publish fourteen books of 'Retractations', it is not likely but that I have,
in the following pages, erred in some points, at least verbally;
but I am the more likely to be exempt from considerable
error inasmuch as I make no ridiculous pretence of invading
the province of the theologian by defining or explaining
dogma. This I am content with implicitly accepting; my
work being mainly that of the Poet, bent only upon dis-
covering and reporting how the 'loving hint' of doctrine
has 'met the longing guess' of the souls of those who have so
believed in the Unseen that it has become visible, and who
have thenceforward found their existence to be no longer a
sheath without a sword, a desire without fulfilment. The
steam-hammer of that Intellect which could be so delicately
adjusted to its task as to be capable of either crushing a Hume
or cracking a Kingsley is no longer at work, that tongue
which had the weight of a hatchet and the edge of a razor is
silent; but its mighty task of so representing truth as to make
it credible to the modern mind, when not interested in un-

19

belief, has been done. I only report the cry which certain 'babes in Christ' have uttered: 'Taste and see that the Lord is sweet.' And far be it from me to pose as other than a mere reporter, using the poetic intellect and imagination so as in part to conceive those happy realities of life which in many have been and are an actual and abiding possession; and to express them in such manner that thousands who lead beautiful and substantially Catholic lives, whether outside or within the visible Church, may be assisted in the only true learning, which is to know better that which they already know.

I should be horrified if a charge of 'originality' were brought against me by any person qualified to judge whether any of the essential matter of this book were 'original' or not. Mine is only a feeble endeavour to 'dig again the wells which the Philistines have filled'. I am quite aware that many readers, zealously Christian, will put aside this little volume with a cry of 'Ugh, ugh! the horrid thing; it's alive!' My book is perhaps open to this objection, but there is no help for it.

It may also be objected that there is no particular reason for the limits I have set myself in this volume. There might just as well have been three volumes as one, or thirty as three. I have not written more, simply because, in some matters, a part is greater than the whole, a little more than much; and the thoughts which the reader may be induced by what I have written to think for himself, will be a hundred-fold more valuable to him if so learned than if they were learned from me.

A systematic Philosopher, should he condescend to read the following notes, will probably say, with a little girl of mine to whom I showed the stars for the first time, 'How untidy the sky is!' But who does not know that all philosophies have had to pay, for the blessing of system, by the curse of barrenness? Sensible people will feel shocked at my 'paradoxes', which, however, are not mine, and are, as Coleridge says, the only mode in which realities of a certain order can be approximately expressed. The readers from whom alone I expect a full and hearty, though silent, welcome, are those literary persons who, I am sincerely glad to see, find my writing, as Fuseli said of Blake, 'D——d good to steal from', not knowing the sources from which I also have derived my matter—and make it my only claim to be heard that I have done so.

Lymington, May 1895.

AUREA DICTA

AUREA DICTA

I

IF YOU WISH TO INFLUENCE THE world for good, leave it, forget it, and think of nothing but your own interests.

II

'He must have very little spirit', says St. Bernard, 'who thinks that a spirit is nothing.'

III

'God', says a great Philosopher—Proclus, if I remember rightly—'is not infinite, but the synthesis of Infinite and Boundary.'

IV

All reasoning ends in an appeal to self-evidence.

V

That which is absolutely simple, the Life, which is the root or *surd* of all, must be literally *absurd*. Let us concede this point to the scientist.

VI

If you try to simplify or pare off the superfluous from the minds and speech of most men, you will find that nothing is left. There is *no* simplicity in them, for there is no truth: truth and simplicity being, as Aquinas says, the same thing.

VII

'He who meditates night and day upon the law of the Lord shall yield his fruit in due season.'

VIII

Heaven, Earth, Sea, and Hell witness with a thousand voices the secret which is the sole felicity of man; and almost all men refuse to hear.

IX

'Searchers of Majesty shall be overwhelmed with the glory.' Blissfully overwhelmed; ruined for this world, yet even in this enriched beyond thought; happy searchers, consumed by the thunder of divine instructions and the lightning of divine perceptions, but surviving as a new creature in the very flesh of her destroyer.

X

With unscaled eye-balls I beheld the Rod,
And in the garden walk'd again with God,
says Browning. Let him whose eyes have been thus opened
beware; for none is ever restored to Paradise a *second* time.

XI

When a thing manifestly *is*, none but fools will trouble
themselves with difficulties as to *how* it can be. And yet who
is not more or less a fool? Who dares to believe his own eyes?

XII

The spirit of man is like a kite, which rises by means of those
very forces which seem to oppose its rise; the tie that joins
it to the earth, the opposing winds of temptations, and the
weight of earth-born affections which it carries with it into
the sky.

XIII

Lovers put out the candles and draw the curtains, when they
wish to see the god and the goddess; and in the higher
Communion, the night of thought is the light of perception.

XIV

Greatly to live is such a burthen of joy that the sharpest pain
of sacrifice is a welcome easement of it. 'Consummatum est.'
The Cross is only a mitigation of the consummation.

XV

Hate pleasure, if only because this is the only means of obtaining it. Reject the foul smoke, and it will be forced back on you as pure flame. But this you cannot believe, until you shall have rejected it without thought of reward.

XVI

Great is his faith who dares believe his own eyes.

XVII

Nature fulfilled by grace is not less natural, but is supernaturally natural.

XVIII

The promises of the Devil are kept to the letter and broken in the spirit; God's promises are commonly broken to the letter and fulfilled past all hope to the spirit.

XIX

Man, looking on that which is below him, is an 'image' of God, and knows not but that he is God; but, looking upwards, he becomes a 'likeness' of God, as the sheath is the likeness of the sword.

XX

There are not two sides to any question that really concerns a man, but only one; and this side only a fool can fail to see if he tries.

XXI

No writer, sacred or profane, ever uses the words 'he' or 'him' of the soul. It is always 'she' or 'her'; so universal is the intuitive knowledge that the soul, with regard to God who is her life, is feminine.

XXII

Science is a line, art a superficies, and life, or the knowledge of God, a solid.

XXIII

The Tree of Knowledge is become, to the chosen, the Tree of Life; 'Under the Tree where thy mother was debauched I have redeemed thee'.

XXIV

Rhea, the Earth, was the mother of the Gods, and it is only by inspired knowledge of our own nature, or earth, which is seen, that we can know anything of the Divine, which is unseen. 'The natural first, afterwards the supernatural.'

XXV

No great art, no really effective ethical teaching can come from any but such as know immeasurably more than they will attempt to communicate.

XXVI

We often mistake our own sweet childhood for the old time, which, had we lived in it, we should have found almost as intolerable as our own. The world has always been the dunghill it is now, and it only exists to nourish, here and there, the roots of some rare, unknown, and immortal Flower of individual humanity.

XXVII

Do the right, and God will enable you to do it rightly.

XXVIII

So give me to possess this mystery that I shall not desire to understand it.

XXIX

Our thoughts and feelings are modifications of our spiritual substance, and the soul, as a phonograph, retains them all forever, to lie tacit or to be summoned at need.

##

Ask abundantly, for the measure of your asking shall be that of your receiving.

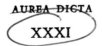

XXXI

'An instant of pure love is more precious to God and the soul, and more profitable to the Church than all other good works together, though it may seem as if nothing were done.'—*St. John of the Cross.*

XXXII

God loves the soul which desires perfection, as a Lover always does, that is as if she were already perfect. The fact creates, when apprehended, a far more vehement desire to become perfect than if perfection were the price of such love in the future.

XXXIII

'What you do not understand, with submission wait for, and what you do understand, hold fast with charity.'—*St. Augustine.*

XXXIV

'Then Tobias exhorted the Virgin and said to her: For these three nights we are joined to God; and when the third night is over, we will be in our own wedlock.'

XXXV

God sets the soul long, weary, impossible tasks, yet is satisfied by the first sincere proof that obedience is intended, and takes the burden away forthwith. 'Could ye not watch with me one hour?'

XXXVI

None attains the promised land 'except those little ones who ye said should be a prey', i.e. the perceptions attained in and preserved from childhood and youth, which the Tempter is always endeavouring to destroy.

XXXVII

To some there is revealed a sacrament greater than that of the Real Presence, a sacrament of the Manifest Presence, which is, and is more than, the sum of all the sacraments.

XXXVIII

The Catholic Church alone teaches as matters of faith those things which the thoroughly sincere person of every sect discovers, more or less obscurely, for himself, but does not believe, for want of external sanction.

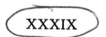

XXXIX

If we may credit certain hints contained in the lives of the Saints, love raises the spirit above the sphere of reverence and worship into one of laughter and dalliance; a sphere in which the Soul says:

> Shall I, the gnat, which dances in Thy ray,
> Dare to be reverent?

XL

God is infinite: all else is indefinite, except woman, who alone is finite, and in her God and all things find their repose. She is *Regina Coeli*, as well as *Regina Mundi*.

XLI

God usually answers our prayers according rather to the measure of His own magnificence than to that of our asking; so that we often do not know His boons to be those for which we besought Him.

XLII

Men would never offend God if they knew how ready He is to forgive them.

XLIII

The sweetness even of self-denial wears with time, and becomes tediously easy.

XLIV

'To do good and truth *for the sake of good and truth* is to love the Lord above all things and one's neighbour as oneself.'

XLV

Divine favours are forced upon the Soul in proportion to her detachment from them.

XLVI

It is one thing to be blind, and another to be in darkness.

XLVII

Pardon is not over and done with once for all, but incessant contrition and incessant pardon are the compensating dainties of those in heaven who have lost the dainties of first innocence.

XLVIII

In times of darkness and temptation the influx of blessing from God is not stopped but only checked in its course, as by a dam, and the longer the temptation the greater the flood of good that pours in from Him who then 'Turns our captivity as the Rivers in the South'.

XLIX

'To him that waits all things reveal themselves', provided that he has the courage not to deny, in the darkness, what he has seen in the light.

L

When first you unite yourself by charity to the whole human race, then shall you indeed perceive that Christ died for you.

LI

Delight is pleasanter than pleasure; peace more delightful than delight. 'Seek peace and ensue it.'

LII

Creation differs from subsistence only as the first leap of a fountain differs from its continuance.

LIII

When once the ponderous wheel of the will is set in motion towards God, the same pressure, steadily applied, will increase its speed indefinitely.

LIV

The modern Agnostic improves upon the ancient by adding 'I don't care' to 'I don't know'.

LV

A moment's fruition of a true felicity is enough and eternity not too much.

LVI

You shall never recover in heaven the least good which you have profaned and forfeited by seeking it consciously against order. You may, by great repentance, get something better, but never that.

LVII

The wilful brook of man's nature desires to go by rule, and chafes at all that checks its straight course; the sea of grace fills by turns every changing dimple in the sand, meeting unequal claims with equal duty.

LVIII

All the love and joy that a man has ever received in perception is laid up in him as the sunshine of a hundred years is laid up in the bole of the oak.

LIX

'Let each man', says St. Paul, 'abound in his own sense.' When once he has got into the region of perception let him take care that his vision is his own, and not fancy he can profit himself or others much by trying to appropriate *their* peculiar variations of the common theme.

LX

The Angels, it is said, fell, because they would not obey the command that, at the name of Jesus every knee in Heaven and Earth should bow. They were too pure! And it is by the Devil's purity that many angelic spirits are prevented from attaining Heaven.

LXI

The only *evidence* to which the Church appeals is *self-evidence*. To the sane and simple mind all serviceable truth is self-evident, on being simply asserted. The Gospel of Christ is merely 'good news'.

LXII

The ardour chills us which we do not share.

LXIII

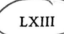

The more wild and incredible your desire the more willing and prompt God is in fulfilling it, if you will have it so.

LXIV

The religion of most persons who are sincerely religious is in a state of fire-mist, which a due meditation on the Incarnation would condense into New Heavens and a New Earth.

LXV

Your dunghill fowl is not in the least embarrassed if he finds a diamond on his feeding-ground. He knows its exact value for *him*, and kicks it out of his way with a crow of exultation at the clearness of his own discernment.

LXVI

Would you possess what is, and shun what seems? Believe and cling to nothing but your dreams.

LXVII

There are some sorts of love which are permitted only to God. He alone, for instance, may love and worship images graven by His own hands.

LXVIII

It is easy to love when we feel that we are worthy of love, impossible otherwise. A perfect intention, failing only through ignorance, is alone worthiness.

LXIX

That which you confess to-day, you shall perceive to-morrow.

LXX

'In the mouth of two witnesses shall all things be established.' One witness is human instinct inspired by God; the other is the sanction and corroboration of the Church.

LXXI

Woman, according to the *Salve Regina*, is 'Our Life, our Sweetness, and our Hope'. God is so only in so far as He is 'made flesh', i.e. Woman. 'The Flesh of God is the Head of Man', says St. Augustine. Thus the Last is indeed the First. 'The lifting of her eyelash is my Lord.'

38

Tennyson

LXXII

The obligatory dogmata of the Church are only the seeds of life. The splendid flowers and the delicious fruits are all in the corollaries, which few, besides the Saints, pay any attention to. Heaven becomes very intelligible and attractive when it is discerned to be—Woman.

LXXIII

Great contemplatives are infallible, so long as they only affirm. When they begin to prove, any fool can confute them.

LXXIV

A thing harder, to those who love, than actual sacrifice is to submit to the greatness of God's beneficence towards us. His promises so far exceed our power of desiring, that we cling to limitations, not discerning that, whatever form the unknown felicity of His Chosen may take, and however far beyond our present capacity it may be, it must include all the felicity and fidelity of limitation to which we now cleave.

LXXV

It becomes a fact of *experience* to those who truly live, that not only must we give up *all* in order to obtain all, but that we must do so before we attain to any assurance that such will be our reward. Where, otherwise, would be the sacrifice?

LXXVI

Many a Lover must have said to himself, 'There are sufferings far worse than hanging for a few hours upon a Cross. What is that, beside the fact that one's destined Bride is in another's bed?' But has not Christ suffered this? Lies not the Soul, the Miranda of His desires, contented in the bed of Caliban, so long as she prefers the world to Him?

LXXVII

'O Anima naturaliter Christiana!' exclaimed Tertullian.

LXXVIII

'Enthusiasm' is a foul mockery of pure zeal. True goods are peacefully desired, sought without eagerness, possessed without elation, and postponed without regret.

LXXIX

'They are under the auspices of the Lord and led by His good pleasure with whom He dwells in ultimates.'

LXXX

Some saint has written: 'Love not only levels but subjects; and the Soul that is truly the Bride of God cannot ask anything without getting it, though it should be to her own injury.'

LXXXI

They who ask for no sign shall have many.

LXXXII

'See that thou tell no man.' When our Lord gives vision to the Soul, He always speaks this command to the conscience.

LXXXIII

All the world is secretly maddened by the mystery of love, and continually seeks its solution everywhere but where it is to be found.

LXXXIV

Direct teaching cannot go much beyond pointing out the conditions of perception, and the direction in which it is to be looked for.

LXXXV

Consider what is the most marked characteristic of the popular literature and art of the present time, and think whether it is not exactly to be described as 'the abomination of desolation in the *holy places*'.

LXXXVI

'The human form divine.' It is *actually* divine; for the Body is the house of God, and an image of Him, though the Devil may be its present tenant.

LXXXVII

'Each particular perception gives rise to a perceptive state, the permanence of which is memory.'—*Aristotle*. So that the man's life is the sum of his perceptions, and of his inferences from them, which are themselves perceptions.

LXXXVIII

Belief in the Incarnation *is* immortality, for it really subsists only with those in whom the Incarnation already is. 'None can say that Jesus is the Lord but by the Holy Ghost.'

LXXXIX

'Under the Tree where thy mother was debauched, I have redeemed thee.' 'We are healed by the serpent by which we were slain.' It is by the natural desires that we were slain, and it is by the natural desires, made truly natural by inoculation with the Body of Christ, that we are ultimately saved. Religion has no real power until it becomes *natural*.

XC

Goethe said that 'God is manifested in ultimates'; that is, in facts of human nature of which we not only see no explanation, but also see that no explanation is possible.

XCI

Adam's naming of the animals in Paradise was his vision of the nature, distinction, and purpose of each of his own instincts and powers: for *he* was paradise.

XCII

The bliss of heaven, which many have attained here, is the synthesis of absolute content and infinite desire.

XCIII

'We are saved by hope'; but how shall we hope without some knowledge of what to hope for?

XCIV

The most pregnant passages of Scripture, of the wise ancients, and of great poets are those which seem to you to have no meaning, or an absurd one.

XCV

A dark, conspicuous, and insoluble enigma is the source of all love, and of the celestial decorum of the universe.

XCVI

What a Lover sees in the Beloved is the projected shadow of his own potential beauty in the eyes of God. The shadow is given to those who cannot see themselves in order that they may learn to believe the word: 'Rex concupiscet decorem tuum.'

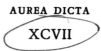

XCVII

'Detachment' consists, not in casting aside all natural loves and goods, but in the possession of a love and a good so great that all others, though they may and do acquire increase through the presence of the greater love and good, which explains and justifies them, seem nothing in comparison.

XCVIII

An hypothesis may be of the greatest help to the mind as showing that a thing is explicable, though the explanation may not be the true one.

XCIX

'One fool will deny more truth in half an hour than a wise man can prove in seven years.'

C

God's Law is the 'ten-stringed harp' of David, and all the music of life resides in the various and measured vibration with which it responds to the touch of the passions. Sin snaps the strings in its ignorant and brutal preference of noise to music.

CI

Nations die of softening of the brain, which, for a long time, passes for softening of the heart.

CII

'Rationalism' begins at the wrong end. Religion rationalises from the primary and substantial Reason, and explains all things. Rationalists take zero for their datum, and, do what they may, they can make nothing of it.

CIII

'*Noli me tangere*' is the only favour which the Saint asks from the world.

CIV

The Holy Spirit so speaks with the divine tongue in each prophet that each man hears Him speak in his own tongue.

CV

No degree of purity is possible to him who does not endeavour to obey the command, 'Be ye pure as I am pure'.

CVI

All men are led to Heaven by their own loves; but these must first be sacrificed.

CVII

The Poet alone has the power of so saying the truth 'which it is not lawful to utter', that the disc with its withering heat and blinding brilliance remains wholly invisible, while enough warmth and light are allowed to pass through the clouds of his speech to diffuse daylight and genial warmth.

CVIII

'The Ark of the Covenant was', says Aquinas, 'a symbol of mysteries of the faith which must not be unveiled but to those who are advanced in holiness.'

CIX

Heaven is too much like Earth to be spoken of, as it really is, lest the generality should think it like their Earth, which is Hell.

CX

The great secrets of life lie too far within, not too far beyond, our mental focus to be seen. Philosophy consists in limiting the focus, not in extending it.

CXI

Nothing can corroborate an ascertained material fact; but spiritual facts are capable of infinite corroboration. The fact of love, for example, is capable of infinite corroboration. This explains the talk and behaviour of lovers.

CXII

It is only by fidelity to truth, which is beyond perception, that perception can be attained and sustained. 'Do my commandments and ye shall know of the doctrine.'

CXIII

The scientist asks, with the father of John the Baptist, 'How shall I know these things?' and the answer is, 'You shall be blind till they come about.'

CXIV

'I tell you these things, not because you know them not, but because ye know them.' All living instruction is nothing but corroboration of intuitive knowledge.

CXV

'Everything which is not of faith is sin.' Nature, without faith, whereby the internal realities of Nature are acknowledged and discerned, is a nut of which the kernel is dust and corruption.

CXVI

'God is infinitely credible', says St. Augustine, that is, He is also infinitely incredible. Modern thought only recognises the latter half of the proposition. But man is sane in proportion as he can say, with David, 'Thy testimonies, O God, are become exceedingly credible'.

CXVII

The power of believing and acting upon self-evidence is true strength of intellect and character.

CXVIII

The account of the Creation in Genesis is prophecy, not history. We are now in the beginning of the Sixth Day. Woman is being created out of man.

CXIX

Not only are all things known by their relatives and contraries, but the capacity for the one is created by the other. Extremity of evil *creates* the capacity for extremity of good, and the existence of evil is thus justified: temporary evil creates capacity for eternal good.

CXX

Contrast, artistic and otherwise, is not between absolute positive and absolute negative, but between different degrees of the same positive. Night would not be a contrast to day, were night really dark.

CXXI

Popular esotericism—and esotericism is becoming popular—means conscientious wenching, or worse.

CXXII

The promises of God are samples of what is promised; as a handful of wheat is of the barn.

CXXIII

'All things are made for the supreme good things, all things tend to that end; and we may be said to account for a thing when we show that it is so best.'—*Berkeley.*

##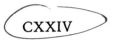

'What ought to be must be.'—*St. Augustine.*

CXXV

Fortunately for themselves and the world, nearly all men are cowards and dare not act on what they believe. Nearly all our disasters come of a few fools having the 'courage of their convictions'.

CXXVI

Nothing hinders progress in the only true knowledge, the real knowledge of God and thence of one's self, so much as the desire to reconcile one reality of perception with another. We should go on extending our apprehension of realities without regard to seeming contradictions, which will disappear of themselves in time, or, at least, in eternity.

CXXVII

How fair a flower is sown
When Knowledge goes, with fearful tread,
To the dark bed
Of the divine Unknown!

CXXVIII

What the world, which truly knows *nothing*, calls 'mysticism', is the science of *ultimates*, 'in which', as Goethe says, 'God is manifest'; the science of self-evident Reality, which cannot be 'reasoned about', because it is the object of pure reason or perception. The Babe sucking its mother's breast, and the Lover returning, after twenty years' separation, to his home and food in the same bosom, are the types and princes of Mystics.

CXXIX

The most ardent love is rather epigrammatic than lyrical. The Saints, above all St. Augustine, abound in epigrams.

CXXX

Not one good prayer has been composed, either by Catholic or Protestant, since the days of the Reformation. The additions to the Breviary, since the Council of Trent, have no ray of divine insight; and the manuals of devotion compiled since then, by authority or otherwise, are enough to drive a sensible Christian crazy by their extravagance and unreality.

CXXXI

Union must precede conjunction. Conjunction is the fruition, or consciousness, of union.

CXXXII

The power of the Soul for good is in proportion to the strength of its passions. Sanctity is not the negation of passion but its order. (See *Confessions of St. Augustine* and the Letter of St. Bernard on the death of his brother.) Hence great Saints have often been great sinners.

CXXXIII

The woman is the man's 'glory', and she naturally delights in the praises which are assurances that she is fulfilling her function; and she gives herself to him who succeeds in convincing her that she, of all others, is best able to discharge it for *him*. A woman without this kind of 'vanity' is a monster.

CXXXIV

'Faith is the substance of things hoped for, and the evidence (being evident) of things unseen.'

CXXXV

Love is a recent discovery, and requires a new law. Easy divorce is the vulgar solution. The true solution is some undiscovered security for true marriage.

CXXXVI

The holier and purer the small aristocracy of the true Church becomes, the more profane and impure will become the mass of mankind.

CXXXVII

To call Good Evil is the great sin—the sin of the Puritan and the Philistine. To call Evil Good is comparatively venial.

CXXXVIII

Nature will not bear any absolute and sustained contradiction. She must be converted, not outraged; and she can be converted only by the substitution, for the lesser satisfaction, of a greater good in the same kind.

CXXXIX

The worthiest occupation of the Wise, in these days, is to 'dig again the wells which the Philistines have filled'.

CXL

'If the Lord tarry wait for Him, and He will not tarry but will come quickly.' The impatience of the Soul for vision is one of the last faults that can be cured. Only to those who watch and wait, with absolute indifference as to the season of revelation, do all things reveal themselves.

CXLI

All particular knowledge, when fully seen, falls into the one Word—the Word made flesh—the Name which can be uttered only by the Spirit to the spirit, and is incapable of being reported in the parables of the senses, because that Word is the synthesis of all things, and the Sabbatical rest of One Spirit in one sense.

CXLII

Those who know God know that it is quite a mistake to suppose that there are only five senses.

CXLIII

Books are influential in proportion to their obscurity. provided that the obscurity be that of inexpressible Realities, The Bible is the most obscure book in the world. He must be a great fool who thinks he understands the plainest chapter of it. The coming of God is always 'in the clouds of heaven', and an unclouded God would be wholly invisible and inaudible.

CXLIV

The name of God is 'Mundum pugillo continens'. The name of man is 'Deum pugillo continens'.

CXLV

O sane madness, which can find, in the sharpest austerities and troubles a present heaven: O mad sanity, which, in all the pleasures of earth, can find no testimony that there is any heaven at all!

CXLVI

'The soul of the Lover lives in the body of his Mistress', says Plutarch. 'Ye are two in one flesh', says St. Paul. 'My body is already joined to God', says St. Agnes. 'She who loves God is chaste, she who touches Him is clean, she who embraces Him is a virgin indeed', says another great Saint.

CXLVII

The highest and deepest thoughts do not 'voluntary move harmonious number', but run rather to grotesque epigram and doggerel.

CXLVIII

Let none of those comparatively few who have attained to the knowledge of 'the secret of the King', which is nothing less than the supersession of faith by sight, despise those who are still walking by faith only; but let them remember the word of Jesus: 'Because thou hast seen me, Thomas, thou hast believed: blessed are they that have not seen, and have believed.'

CXLIX

God made man 'a little lower than the angels to crown him with the honour and glory' of being His own final and Sabbatical felicity. This would be an incredible condition of happiness for man, had not God made it clear to him in other ways that the fruition of heights is in the depths.

CL

You may see the disc of Divinity quite clearly through the smoked glass of humanity, but no otherwise.

CLI

The Father, the Word, and the Holy Spirit are the three dimensions of God, and the apprehension of Him has no substance or reality without them.

CLII

It is the privilege of the simple and pure to know God when they see Him. All men have seen God, but nearly all call Him by a very different name. The light shineth in darkness, but the darkness comprehendeth it not.

CLIII

Woman desires the infinite, man the finite. She is the continent of the infinite, making it conscious and powerful by limitation.

> 'Tis but in such captivity
> The Heavens themselves know what they be.'

CLIV

Pride does much and ill, Love does little and well.

CLV

'*Taste* and see that the Lord is sweet.' Taste or touch discerns substance. 'It is', says Aristotle, 'a sort of sight', with this difference that it is infallible.

CLVI

The Soul's shame at its own unworthiness of the embraces of God is the blush upon the rose of love, which is the deeper the more angelic her intelligence and consequent discernment of God's purity.

CLVII

A Kempis says: 'He who has not been tried knows nothing.'
This not only because the knowledge of truth and good can
be made a man's own only by bringing it into action when
under temptation, but also because 'all perception of good,
all happiness and felicity are proportionate to the experience
of their opposites'.

CLVIII

Sallust, the Platonist, says: 'The intention of all mystic
ceremonies is to conjoin us with the world and with the
Gods.' Until we are so conjoined by divine, or substantial
knowledge, we know as little of the world as we do of the
Gods.

CLIX

'The ideas of interior thought in man are above material
things, but still they are terminated in them, and where they
are terminated there they appear to be.' God is manifest in
ultimates. 'My Covenant shall be in your flesh.' 'The three
heavens' (celestial, spiritual, and natural) 'are one in ultimates', i.e. the first can stand without the second or third;
the second includes the first but can stand without the third;
the third must include the other two.

CLX

The divinely enlightened imagination is the only means of
apprehending God in His relationships to the Soul, and every
corroborative analogy is an actual and eternally ascertained
approach to that fullness of vision which never can be full.

CLXI

The 'wildest hyperboles' of Love and Poetry are the simplest and truest expressions of the only 'scientific facts' that are worthy to be called science. When a Lover says and means that he has been 'made immortal by a kiss', he states an unexaggerated truth. His immortality, or his capacity for immortality, *has* been increased and partly initiated by the experience; for our eternity is but the sum, simultaneity, explanation, and transfiguration of all our pure experiences in time.

KNOWLEDGE AND SCIENCE

KNOWLEDGE AND SCIENCE

I

IN HIS UNION AND CONJUNCTION with Body, God finds His final perfection and felicity. 'It is not written that He has taken hold of any of the angels; but of us He has taken hold.' 'Deliciæ meæ esse cum filiis *hominum*.' The great prophecy, 'Man shall be compassed by a woman', was fulfilled when Jesus Christ made the body, which He had taken from Mary, actually divine by the subdual of its last recalcitrance upon the Cross. The celestial marriage, in which, thenceforward, every soul that chose could participate, was then consummated. 'Consummatum est', and the Body became—

> Creation's and Creator's crowning good;
> Wall of infinitude;
> Foundation of the sky,
> In Heaven forecast
> And long'd for from eternity,
> Though laid the last.

II

God clothes Himself actually and literally with His whole creation. Herbs take up and assimilate minerals, beasts assimilate herbs, and God, in the Incarnation and its proper Sacrament, assimilates us, who, as St. Augustine says, 'are God's beasts'.

III

'Amen, I say unto you there are some of them that stand here that shall not taste death till they see the Son of Man coming in His Kingdom.' Again, 'I did not say that he should not die, but that he should not die till I come'. To some, not necessarily, perhaps, the greatest saints, Christ is actually and perceptibly risen. He has turned the water of nature into the wine of the Marriage Feast, though 'His time is not yet come', and, to the Sacrament of the Real Presence, He has added a Sacrament of the Manifest Presence. For souls thus favoured, the Church's teaching and rites are but as a scaffolding which has fulfilled its purpose. The Temple is built and occupied. 'Felix quem Veritas per se docet . . . Taceant omnes doctores.' For these alone can such words as the following have any intelligible meaning:

> The Lord for the body, and the body for the Lord.
> God manifest in the reality of our flesh.
> Bear and glorify God in your bodies.
> Shall I take the members of Christ, and make them
>   the members of a harlot?
> The fullness of the Godhead manifested bodily.
> My covenant shall be in your flesh.

IV

The Church regards some degree of *affective*, or sensitive, love as essential to the right receiving of the Holy Eucharist. It must obviously be so, for what is the 'Communion of the Body' but the communion of the sensitive Soul? De Condron says: 'We should communicate, not only for our soul's benefit, but also to satisfy Our Lord's exceeding longing for us.' But we must be able to believe His 'longing for us' in order that we may be able to reciprocate it. Surely the altar-rail is not sufficiently guarded against intruders, who only 'eat to their damnation'.

V

There comes a time in the life of every one who follows the Truth with full sincerity when God reveals to the *sensitive* Soul the fact that He and He alone can satisfy those longings, the satisfaction of which she has hitherto been tempted to seek elsewhere. Then follows a series of experiences which constitute the '*sure* mercies of David'. The Enemy, who can assault us only through the flesh, has had his weapon taken out of his hands. The sensitive nature is, from day to day, refreshed with a sweetness that makes the flesh-pots of Egypt insipid; and the Soul cries 'Cor meum et caro mea exultaverunt in Deum vivum'.

VI

Man's sensitive soul is Paradise and the ultimate felicity of God; and 'To him that overcometh shall be given to eat of the Tree of Life' (God Himself) 'which is planted in the midst of that Paradise'. 'This day', says the Roman Breviary, on the Feast of the Assumption by our Lord of the Body of the Blessed Virgin, 'the Eden of the New Adam' (Christ) 'receives the garden of delights in which the Tree of Life was planted.' 'Deliciae meæ esse cum filiis hominum' (Prov.) 'We are his honey', says St. Augustine.

VII

The shame and confusion of the Bride, which are the dainties
of the Bridegroom, and her own, inasmuch as they are
pleasing to him, are not wanting in that marriage which
includes every felicity:

> Blushes are for shame
> Of such an ineffectual flame
> As ill consumes the sacrifice;

and the highest Angel must be overwhelmed with the
confusion and terror of an intimacy altogether beyond
capacity and comprehension.

VIII

If we would find in God that full satisfaction of all our desires which He promises, we must believe *extravagantly*, i.e. as the Church and the Saints do; and must not be afraid to follow the doctrine of the Incarnation into all its *natural* consequences. Those who fear to call Mary the 'Mother of God' simply do not believe in the Incarnation at all; but we must go further, and believe His word when He rebuked the people for regarding her as exclusively His Mother, declaring that every soul who received Him with faith and love was also, in union with Her, His Mother, the Bride of the Holy Spirit. We must not be afraid to believe that this Bride and Mother, with whom we are identified, is 'Regina Coeli', as well as 'Regina Mundi'; and that this Queen of Heaven and Earth is simply a pure, natural woman; and that one of our own race, and each of us, in union with her, has been made 'a little lower than the angels', in order to be 'crowned with honour and glory' far beyond the honour and glory of the highest of His purely spiritual creatures. 'It is not written that He has taken hold (or united Himself) with any of the angels'; but of the lowest of His spiritual creatures, who alone is also flesh, 'He has taken hold'; and the Highest has found His ultimate and crowning felicity in a marriage of the flesh as well as the Spirit; and in this infinite contrast and intimacy of height with depth and spirit with flesh He, who is very Love, finds, just as ordinary human love does, its final rest and the full fruition of its own life; and the joy of angels is in contemplating, and sharing by perfect sympathy with humanity, that glory which humanity alone actually possesses. This, the literal doctrine of the Church and the Scriptures, sounds preposterous in the ears of nearly all 'Christians' even; and yet its actual truth has been realised, even in this life, as something far more than a credible promise, by those who have received the message of their Angel with somewhat of the faith of Mary, and to each of whom it has been said: 'Blessed art thou because thou hast believed; for there shall be a performance of the things which have been promised to thee.' Let Christians leave off thinking of the Incarnation as a thing past, or a figure of speech, and learn to know that it consists for them in their becoming the intimately and humanly beloved of a divine and yet human Lover; and His local paradise and heaven of heavens.

IX

'My heart is enlarged, I see, I wonder, I abound; my sons come from afar, and my daughters rise up at my side.' This is the knowledge, the *personal* knowledge of God, which immediately follows the first great and uncompromising sacrifice of the Soul to Him. The heart becomes an ocean of knowledge actually perceived. All that previously was confessed by faith is seen far more clearly than external objects are seen by the natural eye. Sons, that is, corroborative truths, come from afar; the most remote facts of past experience and of science are confirmations strong as proofs of Holy Writ; and daughters, all natural affections and desires, find suddenly their interpretation, justification, and satisfaction, and are henceforward as 'the polished corners of the Temple'.

X

When once God 'has made known to us the Incarnation of His Son Jesus Christ by the message of an Angel', that is to say, when once it has become, not an article of abstract faith, but a fact discerned in our own bodies and souls, we are made sharers of the Church's infallibility; for our reasoning is thenceforward from discerned reality to discerned reality, and not from and to those poor and always partially fallacious and misleading signs of realities, thoughts which can be formulated in words. Though he may express himself erroneously, no man, so taught, can be otherwise than substantially orthodox, and he is always willing and glad to submit his expressions to the sole assessor of verbal truth, whose judgments have never been convicted of inconsistency, even by the most hostile and malevolent criticism.

XI

'Eternity', says Aquinas, 'is the entire, simultaneous, and perfect possession of a life without end.' God goes forth from simplicity into all particulars of reality; man returns from all his peculiar and partial apprehensions of reality to God, and *his* eternity is 'the entire, simultaneous, and perfect possession of a life' which is the synthesis of all the real apprehensions, or perceptions of good, which he has acquired here. Hence the acquisition of knowledge is the first business of mortal life—not knowledge of 'facts', but of realities, which none can ever begin to know until he knows that all knowledge but the knowledge of God is vanity.

XII

'God', writes a Persian Poet, 'is at once the mirror and the mirrored, the Lover and the Beloved.' Every Soul was created to be, if it chose, a participator of this felicity, i.e. of 'the glory which the Son had with the Father before the beginning of the world'. *This* is the sum-total of 'mysticism', or true 'science'; and he who has not attained, through denial of himself, to some *sensible* knowledge of this felicity, in reality knows nothing; for all knowledge, worthy of the name, is nuptial knowledge.

XIII

'That which He shows you in secret proclaim on the house-tops'—not to others, but to yourself. The most remote, undefined, and (if you do not fix them in your consciousness, by reflection, affirmation, and corroboration) evanescent thoughts are commonly 'secrets' which are, of all others, the most important and life-affecting.

XIV

'No prophecy is of private interpretation.' We must believe nothing in religion but what has been declared by the Church, but many things declared by the Church must be spoken by the Spirit in the Soul before she can hear them in the word of the Church. Her orthodoxy, then, consists in this, that she must try what she hears in herself by that word, in which all is contained, either explicitly or implicitly. This is not hard, for the one deep calls to the other, and the Spirit knows what the Spirit speaks. Flavour and palate, perfume and nostrils, are not closer correlatives than are revelation and human consciousness.

XV

Plato's cave of shadows is the most profound and simple statement of the relation of the natural to the spiritual life ever made. Men stand with their backs to the Sun, and they take the shadows cast by it upon the walls of their cavern for realities. The shadows, even, of heavenly realities are so alluring as to provoke ardent desires, but they cannot satisfy us. They mock us with unattainable good, and our natural and legitimate passions and instincts, in the absence of their true and substantial satisfactions, break forth into frantic disorders. If we want fruition we must turn our backs on the shadows, and gaze on their realities in God.

It may be added that, when we have done this, and are weary of the splendours and felicities of immediate reality, we may turn again, from time to time, to the shadows, which having thus become intelligible, and being attributed by us to their true origin, are immeasurably more satisfying than they were before, and may be delighted in without blame. This is the 'evening joy', the joy of contemplating God in His creatures, of which the theologians write; and this purified and intelligible joy in the shadow—which has now obtained a core of substance—is not only the hundred-fold 'promise of this life also', but it is, as the Church teaches, a large part of the joy of the blest.

XVI

Knowledge purifies. There are two kinds of impurity: impurity of will, which is sin; and impurity of ignorance, which makes that the Angels themselves are said to be impure in the sight of God. For essential purity is order, and there can be no perfection of order without knowledge of what is the right order of things within us; and the purest of created beings has still to pray 'Order all things in me strongly and sweetly from end to end'. There are in man many floating islands of good, like that of Delos, but he cannot have a perfect conscience concerning them, and they are not safe ground on which to build the temple of God, until they are chained to the bottom of the sea of the senses and perceptions by ordered knowledge. The impurity of ignorance is in none so manifest as in the devout; for they *act* on their ignorance, and fill themselves and others with miserable scruples and hard thoughts of God, and are as apt to call good evil as other men are to call evil good.

XVII

'Unless above himself he can erect himself, how mean a thing is man.' He that sets himself with his whole heart on this task will find at some stage or other of the work that, like Abraham, he has to offer his first born, his dearest possession, his 'ruling love', whatever that may be. He must actually lift the knife—not so much to prove his sincerity to God as to himself; for no man who has not thus won assurance of himself can advance surely. But he will find that he has killed a ram, and that his first-born is safe, and exalted by this offering to be the father of a great nation; and he will understand why God called the place in which this sacrifice was offered 'The land of vision'.

XVIII

What discredits the idea of 'Revelation' most with those who doubt or reject it, is the denial that it is communicated to the whole world. Whereas it is expressly affirmed, in the very first words of St. John's Gospel, that this 'Light lighteth every one that cometh into the world', only they have loved darkness better than light. A *Witness* to a revelation is a different thing: and that religion has the best claims upon us which professes, as Christianity does, to be mainly a Witness of that original and universal light.

XIX

After the main dogmas, which are of faith, the teaching of theologians is very largely derived from facts of psychology within the reach of every one who chooses to pay the cost. For example, one of the most important of these facts is that there are four states or aspects of the Soul towards God; states or aspects which rapidly and inevitably succeed each other, and recur almost daily in the life of every soul which is doing its full duty. The theologians call these states by those times of the day to which they strikingly correspond: Morning, Noon, Evening, and Night. The Morning is the mood of glad, free, and hopeful worship, supplication, and thanksgiving; the Noon is the perfect state of contemplation or spiritual fruition; this cannot be sustained, say the theologians, even by the Angels for very long, and it passes into the 'Evening Joy', in which the Soul turns, not from God, but to God in His creatures—to all natural delights, rendered natural indeed by supernatural insight. Lastly, Night is that condition of the Soul which, in this stage of being, occupies by far the greatest part of the lives even of the most holy, but which will have no existence when the remains of corruption which cause the darkness shall have passed away. 'The wicked', however, 'have no bonds in their death', and this terrible and daily recurring trial is as little known to them as that other after which the 'Bride' sighed: 'Show me where Thou pasturest Thy sheep in the noonday.'

The 'touch' of God is not a figure of speech. 'Touch', says
Aquinas, 'applies to spiritual as well as to material things.'
The same authority says, 'Touch is the sense of alimentation,
taste that of savour'. A perfect life ends, as it begins, in the
simplicity of infancy: it knows nothing of God on whom it
feeds otherwise than by touch and taste. The fullness of
intelligence is the obliteration of intelligence. God is then
our honey, and we, as St. Augustine says, are His; and who
wants to understand honey or requires the *rationale* of a kiss?
The Beatific Vision', says St. Bernard, 'is not seen by the
eyes, but is substance which is sucked as through a nipple.'

XXI

To the living and affirmative mind, difficulties and unintelligibilities are as dross, which successively rises to the surface, and dims the splendour of ascertained and perceived truth, but which is cast away, time after time, until the molten silver remains unsullied; but the negative mind is lead, and, when all its formations of dross are skimmed away, nothing remains.

XXII

I once asked a famous theologian why he did not preach the love and knowledge of God from his pulpit as he had been discoursing of them for a couple of hours with me, instead of setting forth

> Doctrine hard
> In which Truth shows herself as near a lie
> As can comport with her divinity.

He answered that, if he were to do so, his whole congregation would be living in mortal sin before the end of the week. It is true. The work of the Church in the world is, not to teach the mysteries of life, so much as to persuade the soul to that arduous degree of purity at which the God Himself becomes her teacher. The work of the Church ends when the knowledge of God begins.

XXIII

When the state which the theologians call 'Perfection' is attained, and life is from good to truth instead of from truth to good, the connection between truths ceases to be an intellectual necessity. Not only the 'earth', or mass of related knowledge, but 'the multitude of the isles is thine'. Every discerned good is assured truth and safe land, whether its subaqueous connection with the main continent is demonstrable or not. 'Love and do what you like.' 'Habitual grace' knows how to suck the baits off the hooks of the Devil, and can take up adders without being bitten.

XXIV

There is a perfectly simple test by which you may know whether you have attained the region of divine perception. The particular sayings and narratives of Scripture, which have seemed, if we would confess it, the most utter nonsense and absurdity, or mere figures of speech, will gradually become centres of ineffable light, and self-evident truths of being; there will be no more doubt as to your seeing the right meaning than there is about the key that fits the lock, or the answer, when given, to an ingenious enigma; and these sayings and narratives, from being habitually passed over as hopelessly unmeaning or as 'Eastern' hyperboles and *façons de parler*, will carry henceforward the only instructions worth listening to.

XXV

Bacon and Macaulay both charged Plato with being occupied by words, not things; as if the words of Plato were not often things, at once the topmost flowers and the fruits of that Tree, both of Life and Knowledge, of which the roots are forever hidden in the speechless depths. A man may read Plato without clearly comprehending much of what he means. He cannot read him without becoming, in some degree, a changed man. But he may read and understand every line that Lord Macaulay ever wrote, without any other profit than that of having extended his acquaintance with historical facts, and having become, perhaps, a clearer writer and speaker. The same authorities bring the same charge, namely, that of being mere players upon words, against Aquinas and all the Schoolmen; whereas, to a man who feels that there can be nothing worthy of interest in comparison with himself, the *Summa* of St. Thomas must be the most real and interesting of books; for it contains hundreds and hundreds of perfectly clear, self-evident, and final definitions of things, for want of being clear about which many men, and those the best, find their thoughts and ways beset with scruples and difficulties. Twenty years before I saw my way to the adoption of any fixed creed, the *Summa* was to me the most delightful and profitable of reading; and I think that I am less than most men given to mistaking words for things.

86

XXVI

Every evil is some good spelt backwards, and in it the wise
know how to read Wisdom. 'Destruction and Death say, we
have heard the fame thereof', and Life says, 'Memor ero
Rahab et Babylonis scientium me'; and 'one extreme', says the
Philosopher, 'is known by another'.

.

XXVII

The Pagan who simply believed in the myth of Jupiter, Alcmena, and Hercules, much more he who had been initiated into the unspeakable names of Bacchus and Persephone, knew more of living Christian doctrine than any 'Christian' who refuses to call Mary the 'Mother of God'.

XXVIII

'Science' makes a boast of death, and the dryness of its bones; but it is working for a day of which it little dreams, when the Spirit shall summon these together with a mighty blast, and shall clothe them with flesh; and such as loved death shall stand aghast, receiving, as all men do in the end, that which they have chosen.

XXIX

A large proportion of the difficulties which many people find in the way of faith arise from their identification of the idea of substance with that of matter, which is only one kind of substance. They forget that science is certainly acquainted with at least one kind of substance which is not matter, and which has none of the properties of matter, I mean ether. What hinders, then, that there should be many kinds of substance, each more subtle than that below it, as ether is more subtle than matter; and why not correspondent ranges of being, until you reach the absolute and underivative substance, God?

XXX

The modern Catholic looks on, with serenity, at the advances
of physical science, ready to admit and glad to make use of
all its permanent discoveries, and to confess that they may
greatly modify or possibly invalidate, not Revelation, but
some practically unimportant points in the customary
reading of the letter of Revelation. He is, however, naturally
somewhat contemptuous of, and indignant at, the shameless
effrontery of physicists in setting forth hypotheses as established truths, and the equally shameless abandonment of
them, without apology, when they have fallen, as most of
the most famous and, for the time, infallible theories have
done, before a fuller knowledge. The modern physicist, as a
rule, is always girding at Christianity as if he had an obscure
conviction that it held the clues to the mysteries which he is
always and vainly endeavouring to fathom. Considering his
exclusive devotion to phenomena, I wonder that the pheno-
menon of a Faraday, at once the greatest of modern physicists
and one of the simplest of Christians, has not exercised his
curiosity more than it has done, or that such curiosity should
not have been also arrested by the fact that the incomparable
galaxy of scientific men who were the founders and early
members of the Royal Society were all (if I remember
rightly) fervent believers, in a time when Christianity was
as much ridiculed and hated by choice spirits as it is in our
own. It cannot be said that it was for want of a critical

spirit. Hume and Voltaire do not lose by comparison with Professor Huxley and Mr. John Morley. Nor can it be said that the increase of knowledge of Nature has been so great as much to modify the externals of faith. The history of creation, regarded by some in very early ages as probably 'mythical', has, indeed, been proved to be certainly so, but the myth includes teaching of much more significance to us than the supposed history, and every one should be glad to discover this additional proof that the aim of the writers of Scripture was not to satisfy an idle curiosity about facts which do not concern us. The doctrine of evolution promises to be of very easy assimilation by the Church; and recent considerations on the nature of 'matter' and 'substance' have made the doctrine of the 'Real Presence' much more naturally credible than it could have seemed at the time of the Council of Trent.

XXXI

Exclusive study of material facts seems to lead to an absolute *hatred* of life. 'Ecrasez l'infame' is the cry of modern science. Darwin admitted that 'fact-grinding' had destroyed his imagination, and made him 'nauseate Shakespeare'. Goethe thanked Heaven for saving him from the danger he was once in of being 'shut up in the charnel-house of science'. Coleridge spoke gratefully of Boehme and some other poor mystics for helping to keep his heart from being withered by 'facts'. Profligacy and science (in its modern acceptation) bring about the same destruction of the higher faculties, and by essentially the same means, i.e. by dwelling continually on surfaces and ignoring substance.

XXXII

Science, without the idea of God, as the beginning and end of knowledge, is as the empty and withered slough of the snake, and the man, however 'wise and learned' and 'well conducted', who has freed himself in thought from the happy bondage of that idea, is among the most sordid of slaves, and viler and more miserable than the most abandoned profligate who is vexed by a conscience, or even a superstition. The latter, though miserable, is still alive; but the former is dead, and feels 'no bonds in his death'.

XXXIII

I have said elsewhere that by far the worthiest use of
natural science is in its provision of similes and parables,
whereby the facts of higher knowledge are approximately
expressed and their 'infinite credibility' corroborated by
lower likenesses. After the word which the triple state of
worm, chrysalis, and butterfly supplies for the triple condition of the soul in its states of 'nature', 'grace', and 'glory',
there is no such parabolic speech as that of the qualities of the
common magnet. Obvious fact, insoluble mystery, existence
owing to contact with a greater power of the same kind,
two opposed forces manifest in numerically one substance,
rejection of its similar and desire for its likeness, power of
propagating that living and alluring opposition in an otherwise neutral body and, as it were, 'under the ribs of death',
and, in exact proportion to its own force, positive producing
and exalting negative or negative positive—what is all this
but the echo of the senseless rock to the very voice of far-off
Love, and the effect of the kiss of God transmitted through
the hierarchies of heaven and earth to the lips of the least of
beings? Man (*homo*) is a great magnet, half-way between the
greatest and the least. The male is the positive pole, the female
the negative, and their attraction is the whole force of life,
and their conjunction its whole fire and felicity. And, from
man, we may rise to an almost concrete idea of God, who
made man in His own image, and whom the Church

declares to be 'an Act', the Act of primary Love, the 'embrace', as the Church styles it, of the First and Second Persons, that embrace being the proceeding Spirit of universal Life.

XXXIV

I have been charged with being an 'authoritarian' rather than a 'scientist'. Let anyone examine himself as to how much of his practical knowledge is derived from authority, and how much from 'science', and, unless he has reduced his soul to the dimensions of an insect, he will have to confess that he is also an authoritarian, and that what he knows with scientific certainty is as nothing compared with the practical cer tainties, which he has derived from past and present authority. What can the mass of mankind ('mainly fools', as Carlyle says) know, if they know it not by authority? Even their smattering of 'scientific certainty' is derived almost wholly from faith in the reports of those who are supposed to know more of the matter than others do. Purity, honour, love, fidelity, everything that makes a man a man, are 'the flowers of olden sanctities', are parts of traditional and hereditary faith in the words and characters of those very few who have been inspired with original knowledge, or 'inspiration', and who have consequently spoken with convincing authority and not as the scribes.

XXXV

People believe and cling to a religion, not because they have been taught that certain facts, dogmas, and rites are true, and ought to be held and performed, but for what they find by actual experience they can get by so believing and so doing. The Greeks believed ardently, because their Myths and Mysteries were found to be effectual means of their becoming participators of a higher life than that of Nature; and they were right in killing Socrates for trying to cut off their soul's ordinary food, without offering any substitute. I believe Christianity primarily, because it gives me, in still greater abundance and perfection, what I want and must have. If Mr. Huxley will offer me something yet more substantial, I will accept that; but, in the meantime, it is of no use to set me down to a Barmecide's Feast, which is not even bran, and to tell me that I do not know how I came by my bread and butter. I believe and am sure that the doctrine of the Incarnation, as held by the Church, is not only reasonable, but *certainly* true; but, if I saw the strongest intellectual causes of doubt, I would shut my eyes to them more closely than a man would to evidences against his mother's chastity; for would not a lie, that is at least present life to me, be better than truth that, by its own confession, has no immortality in it, and, in the present, is but dust and ashes?

XXXVI

A strange age of 'Science' in which no one pays the least attention to the one thing worth knowing—himself! No supernatural light is needed to see that 'we are fearfully and wonderfully made', and to enable us to say, with David, 'Such knowledge is too wonderful for me. I cannot attain unto it'. We cannot, indeed, attain to the fullness of it, for the wonder is inexhaustible, and 'the Angels themselves seek to look into these things'; but it is no reason for despising riches that they are inexhaustible, or for diligently gathering sticks and stones because the gold and rubies on the ground are more than we can carry away. It was not always so. 'Scire teipsum' was the maxim of all ancient philosophy, and the stupidest little Greek knew more of Man, and therefore of God, who is 'very Man', than Bacon, and all our 'men of Science', as such since him, put together. We have had only one psychologist and human physiologist—at least, only one who has published his knowledge—for at least a thousand years, namely Swedenborg ('the man of ten centuries', says Coleridge), and he, Mr. Huxley may perhaps think it sufficient to answer, was mad! Perhaps some degree of madness is needed, in modern times, in order so far to save a man from the deadly contagion of their sanity, 'which imagineth evil as a law', as to enable him to open his eyes to the self-evident truths even of natural life.

HOMO

HOMO

I

'WOMAN', SAYS AQUINAS, 'was created apart, in order
that the distinction of sexes' (in the *homo*) 'might be the
better marked, and in order that the man and the woman
herself' (who is also a potential *homo*, or entire humanity)
'might be induced to attend above all to that which is their
worthiest contemplation', i.e. the reflection in themselves of
the nature of God, whereby, as the Church says, 'He has
fruition in Himself'. Hence, in heaven and sometimes even
on earth, the separation ceases; man and woman having
each become the fully conscious *homo*, or duality of sex in
one being, and a real image of Him who said, 'Let us make
Man in *our* image'. The external man and woman are each
the projected *simulacrum* of the latent half of the other, and
they do but love themselves in thus loving their opposed
likenesses.

II

The body, concerning which Science confessedly knows so little—probably because Science has never recognised the clue to its constitution—seems to be expressly formed for that cohabitation and communion of two Persons (whose union is a third) which Scripture and the Church declare that it is made for: 'The Body for the Lord, and the Lord for the Body'; 'I in you and you in me'. There are two brains, in which Science has traced the separate indwelling of the legislative and executive functions, two systems of nerves, active and sentient, two sides of the body, obscurely but decidedly distinguished in their activities, two souls with two consciences, the rational and emotional, a heart with a double and contrasted action, and endless other dualities and reciprocities which are very far from being explained on the score of mere adaptation to external use; and withal a unity arising from co-operation which makes the body itself as clear an echo of the Trinity as the soul is. 'Let *us* make Man in *our* likeness.' Hence, the Catholic Church, which alone of all Churches teaches the Incarnation as a present reality, attaches the first importance to the preservation of the sanctity and purity of the body, as actually the 'House of God'.

To those who look on things as they really are, and not as mere passive habit has made them appear, there is, in this conception, no difficulty beyond such as Nature, in the production of double-sexed plants and animals, has not dispelled. Indeed, it seems to me that the indwelling of two persons in one flesh but in separate bodies—which is not a doctrine but a fact for those who have experienced and observed love—is by far the greater mystery of the two.

The body, as well as the soul, must remain in congeries of mysteries so long as its destiny is not fulfilled; but, as man interprets woman to herself, so God interprets man, who truly leads his natural life only when it becomes supernatural; as thousands upon thousands have experienced. We are 'fearfully and wonderfully made'; and when the truth first flashed upon Jacob: 'This is verily the House of God', well might he add: 'Depart from me, O Lord; for I am a sinful man.' The highest Angel is not worthy of the honours that are showered upon the humblest soul.

III ✓

Nothing is so fatal to that 'real apprehension' which is the life of truth, as thinking about the 'infinite'. Truth must be intelligible to be influential. Our Lord's sufferings cease to impress us if we think of them as infinite, and the bliss of heaven itself requires the idea of limit to make it attractive. I was much helped, on reading the other day—I think in St. Thomas Aquinas—that some attain, in this life, to degrees of felicity beyond the felicity of some who are already in heaven. *Our* God is very Man, and we can know nothing of Him but in so far as He is mirrored in our own humanity. Hence the Church maintains that the supreme wisdom is to meditate continually on the Incarnation, which is limitation.

IV

The Angels gain credibility and human sympathy from the doctrine of their defect of absolute purity; and nothing has made the idea of the Blessed Virgin so amiable in my sight as the saying of St. Augustine that the only sin she is chargeable with is a little vanity in the consciousness of being the Bride and Mother of God. *O felix culpa,* without which she would not have been a woman! If we must think of the Infinite, the most profitable way is to think of God as having made Himself infinitely small, a mere babe sucking a woman's breast, to suit Himself to the smallness of our capacities. Doubtless, the Beggar Maid, like other little Mistresses of great Lovers, did not love him for his greatness, but because he was not too great to kiss her, and to love to hear her sigh 'Darling!' as little maids do, in such circumstances, matching thus, by the greatness of their innocent audacity, the unguessed greatness of their spouses.

> For, ah! who can express
> How full of bonds and simpleness
> Is God;
> How narrow is He,
> And how the wide, waste field of possibility
> Is only trod
> Straight to His homestead in the human heart;
> Whose thoughts but live and move
> Round Man; Who woos his will
> To wedlock with His own, and does distil
> To that drop's span
> The attar of all rose-fields of all love!

V

Who, except, perhaps, Hegel, has ever noted, except by
way of poetical metaphor, the surprising fact, simply natural
and of general experience, of the double and reciprocal
consciousness of love; that marvellous state in which each of
two persons in distinct bodies perceives sensibly all that the
other feels in regard to him or herself, although their
feelings are of the most opposite characters; and this so
completely, each discerning and enjoying the distinct desire
and felicity of the other, that you might say that in each was
the fullness of both sexes. To note one such human fact as
this is to exalt life to fuller consciousness, and to do more for
true science than to discover a thousand new suns.

VI

Nothing more clearly proves that love between man and woman is 'a great sacrament' than the sense of infinite non-desert and infinite poverty of capacity for its whole felicity, which those who are most deserving and most capable of its joy, feel in the presence of its mysteries. From this sense of incapacity for an infinite honour and felicity proceeds the tender passion of refusal, which is the first motion of perfect love, and which it would be adultery to feel towards more than one. The lower love, being the sacrament and substantial shadow of the higher—for in divine things, shadows are substances—is, no less than the higher, ineffable and beyond analysis.

VII

St. Augustine writes that 'Jesus Christ is the Bride as well as
the Bridegroom; for He is the Body', a saying confirmed by
St. Paul's 'Nevertheless the man is not without the woman;
but let God be all in all'; and by St. John of the Cross, who
says, that, at great heights of contemplation, it is possible to
love the Son with the love of the Father—whose love is the
love of a Bridegroom—and furthermore by the great myth
of Teiresias who, at the end of his first seven years of trans-
formation, again ascended the mountain heights of vision,
and recovered his first condition. This wonderful doctrine of
such a reduplicated reciprocity as the natural mind, even
when supernaturally enlightened, can with difficulty receive,
is necessarily involved in the truth that Our Lord and the
regenerated Soul are two in one Body. 'Such knowledge',
cries David, 'is too excellent for me: I cannot attain unto it.'

VIII

Creation is nothing but a concerted piece, consisting of representative repetitions and variations of and harmonious commentaries upon the simple theme, God, who is defined by St. Thomas as an *Act*—the Act of love, the 'embrace' of the First and Second Persons, and their unity is the thence proceeding Spirit of Life, 'Creator Spiritus', the Life and Joy of all things. In this divine contrapuntal music, plagues, the sack of cities, and hell itself (according to St. Augustine) are but discords necessary to emphasise, exalt, and illustrate the harmony. If Beethoven and Bach are but senseless noise to the untrained ears of the boy who likes to hear Balfe on the street organ; you, though you may be capable of Beethoven and Bach, should hesitate to affirm that the sphere-music is not music because to your ears it is nothing but confusion. The first step towards becoming able to hear it is, to fix your attention, as every listener to learned music does, upon the *theme,* which is God, and *'the love which is between Himself'*, the love of which all other loves are more or less remote echoes and refrains. This 'dry doctrine' of the Trinity, or primary Act of Love, is the keynote of all living knowledge and delight. God Himself becomes a concrete object and an intelligible joy when contemplated as the eternal felicity of a Lover with the Beloved, the Anti-type and very original of the Love which inspires the Poet and the thrush.

IX

Man, when he is in health and order of soul and body, is Mount Olympus, and in him, so long as he confesses that he is nothing in himself, are sensibly apparent the powers and majesties, beauties and beatitudes of all gods and goddesses.

Facsimile of Coventry Patmore's handwriting.

The Rod the Root and the Flower.

~~The Rod the Bud and the Flower~~

"There shall come forth a
rod out of the root of Jesse,
and a flower shall rise up
out of his root."
= ~~Isaiah XI. I.~~
"My covenant shall be in your flesh"

By

Coventry Patmore.

London: George Bell & Sons
York Street, Covent Garden.
1895.

Facsimile of Coventry Patmore's handwriting.

X

Woman is the sum and complex of all nature, and is the *visible* glory of God. The divine manhood, indeed, may be *discerned* in man through the cloud of that womanhood of which he is a participator, inasmuch as he also is the Body, which, as St. Augustine says, 'is the Bride'. The 'Word made Flesh' is the word made Woman, and therefore, as that Word constantly affirms, we can know or discern the First Person only through the Second; and, in the relations of Man and Woman and of Christ and the Soul, it is the common womanhood that is the ground and means of communion of the higher with the lower. At the same time, the actual woman is also 'Homo', and has a subordinate participation in the masculine factor (as he has of the feminine), and it is by this only that she can have communion with him; and, if each were not both, neither could have any comprehension of the other, nor any power of perceiving in the other, that reciprocal desire the consciousness of which is the felicity and bond of love. As it is between Man and Woman, so is it between Christ and Man, who is *His* 'Glory', and between God and Christ, who is God's 'Glory'. The future of the Church depends on its assimilation of this, her all-prevailing, though for the most part obscurely expressed, doctrine. Servants of God we were, under the old Dispensation, 'Sons now we are of God; but what we shall be' is only now beginning to appear. It is because religion is less venerated now than ever, and love more, that it has become permissible to look a little behind the veils which have hitherto concealed these truths from the many, though they have always shone clearly to God's Elect, to whom 'Thy Maker is thy Husband' is no hyperbole or figure of speech.

XI

Lovers are nothing else than Priest and Priestess to each other of the Divine Manhood and the Divine Womanhood which are in God; and as it is not necessary, in order to be an effectual minister of the Sacraments that the Priest should be pure and holy or be qualified otherwise than by a right intention in his act of administration, so the weakest purpose of mutual love, in married partners, is enough to make them effectual ministers to each other of that 'great sacrament', which represents and is in little the union of Christ with the Church. This is the only thought that can make their imperfection bearable.

XII

Man and Woman are as the charcoal poles of the electric light, lifeless in themselves, but, in conjunction, the vehicles of and sharers in the fire and splendour which burst forth from the embrace of the original duality of Love, in the double-tongued flames of Pentecost. They are modes and means of God's fruition of Himself in Nature, and the more they confess and discern their own nullity, the greater will be their share in His power of felicity.

XIII

Saint Paul, who held it best that all men should be as himself, and abstain from the touch of woman, says also, 'Neither is the man without the woman, but, as woman is of the man, so man is by the woman', adding, however, 'but let God be all in all'. These seemingly contradictory and inconsequent words can only be understood by assuming that St. Paul had in view the double nature of the individual 'homo', and its likeness herein to God. The external womanhood is a superfluity and even a hindrance to the Saint. He sees in her only the projected shadow of one half of his own personality, and she is an obstacle to his peace and well-being in the society of the reality. But this thought need not trouble us, who are not Saints, in our domestic felicities.

XIV

Things in Nature which revolt and terrify the natural heart may sometimes not impossibly be images and premonitions of good we dare not think of, in the complex heavens. In the world, how often is Miranda found in the bed of Caliban, 'loving what she fears to look on', when she might have married Ferdinand; and Orlando as often weds Audrey instead of Rosalind. These conjunctions, more horrible to contemplate than any mere sin or mortal disaster, are consummated without shame, and sometimes persisted in seemingly without unhappiness or degradation, Miranda continuing to be Miranda, and Orlando Orlando, with apparent indifference to, or even with a perverse preference for, the horror of their situation. Those alone true psychologists, the originators of the ancient myths, had evidently learned to regard this horror as having some heavenly significance, when they joined Vulcan to Venus, Gods to women, and men to Goddesses. And Christianity, by the mouth of St. Augustine, says: 'Christ is the Bride as well as the Bridegroom.' If the Divine Femininity can find satisfaction in becoming, by the Incarnation, one flesh with man, what marvel that certain Mirandas, representing particular and singular aspects of Divinity, should dote on Calibans?

These particular and singular aspects may be resolved by the great order of the Communion of Saints in beatific vision, though their separate and unsolved representation in mortality, in 'licit' relations between the sexes, is incomparably frightful. There is no horror like 'the wickedness of lawful things'; and Ferdinand should be mercifully judged if, in weakness of faith and finding his Miranda weeping, or still worse, contented, in the arms of Caliban, he turns like Nelson his blind eye to the Commander's signal.

XV

God is the great, *positive* Magnet of the Universe, and whatever, in the Universe, aspires to approach Him must assume the *negative,* the feminine, or passive and receptive aspect. He repels and rejects His own primary aspect. He says to His own: 'Thy Maker is thy Husband.' There are, however, rare heights of contemplation, in which, as St. John of the Cross says: 'Christ is discerned as the Bride, for He is the Flesh.'

XVI

Spirits at will
Can either sex assume, or both.
MILTON.

Where God has given very great faith, He leads His own by the way of the Cross. St. Theresa, for example, was in utter spiritual desolation for fourteen years. But weaker souls, whose faith would fail under such trials, He leads by indulging them with premature delights, and at the appeal of the woman in them, though He says, 'Woman, my time is not yet come', He turns the water of the natural senses into the wine of the spiritual, and fills them with spiritual felicities and consolations which make their path through life more than easy.

XVII

'Prove all things; hold fast that which is good' is not a rule for all, nor for many. Great temptations have been suffered and subdued, and the body brought into order, the soul must have lifted the knife to slay its most precious possession, before she can discern good from evil; but when the good of the body, or 'Nature', has been finally denied and rejected, as having, in itself, nothing good or desirable, then the mind at once acquires an infallible intuition of good, which thenceforth takes the place of truth, which is only a schoolmaster to lead us to the sensible, or *natural* possession of God; and thenceforward our converted Eve, the body, becomes, not a fatal hindrance, but the most happy and effectual 'helpmate' and 'glory' of the Spirit.

XVIII

'I cannot help thinking', said General Gordon, 'that the body has much to do with religion.' Here spoke the man of saintly life, who had attained to an obscure Catholic apprehension, without knowing it, of the mystery which is celebrated in the Feasts of the Assumption and Corpus Christi. And, in answer to the question, 'Is life worth living?' the cynic replies, 'That depends on the *liver*'. He would probably be greatly surprised at hearing that his pun, meant to be wicked, is fully justified by the teaching of St. Thomas Aquinas, who declares that the life of contemplation, which is the discernment of God by the spiritual senses, and which he also declares to be the only 'life worth living', cannot co-exist with any present sensible trouble.

XIX

There is one secret, the greatest of all—a secret which no previous religion dared, even in enigma, to allege fully—which is stated with the utmost distinctness by Our Lord and the Church; though this very distinctness seems to act as a thick veil, hiding the disc of the revelation as that of the Sun is hidden by its rays, and causing the eyes of men to avert themselves habitually from that one centre of all seeing. I mean the doctrine of the Incarnation, regarded not as an historical event which occurred two thousand years ago, but as an event which is renewed in the body of every one who is in the way to the fulfilment of his original destiny.

XX

The spiritual body, into which the bodies of those who love and obey God perfectly are from time to time transfigured, is a prism. The invisible ray of the Holy Spirit, entering its candid substance, becomes divided, and is reflected in a triple and most distinct glory from its own surfaces; and we behold Jesus, the Incarnate Second Person, and Moses (the Father) and Elias (the Holy Ghost) talking with Him. But none will or can 'tell the vision to any man, until Christ be risen' in him; and then it is not necessary to tell it to him. This is the 'bow in the cloud' of man's flesh; the pledge that he shall no more be overwhelmed by the deluge of the senses, which are killed for ever by this vision, as the flame of a tallow candle is killed by the electric light.

XXI

'Nature' is the outcome of the conjunction of reciprocal and complementary forms and forces. Perfume is natural to the nostrils, colours to the eye, the key to the lock, man to woman, God to man. Religion is not religion until it has become, not only natural, but so natural that nothing else seems natural in its presence; and until the whole being of man says, 'Whom have I in heaven, but Thee, and what on earth in comparison of Thee?' and 'To whom shall we go if we leave Thee?' God has no abiding power over even the lower forces of Man's nature, so long as they remain unsatisfied and hostile. He conquers nature only by reconciling it; but all goes smoothly and well when, in the Body of God, 'the highest is reconciled to the lowest', and the flesh-pots of Egypt are become insipid and unnatural to a palate which has tasted apter and sweeter sweets.

XXII

To regard God without particular apprehensions of the imagination, and merely as a Spirit endowed with certain 'attributes', 'C'est anéantir le Christianisme sous prétexte de le purifier', says Fénelon. On the contrary, the contemplation of the mysteries of the Incarnation in the analogies of our own nature is declared by theologians and saints to be the perfection of wisdom. 'Where the *Body* of Christ is, there the eagles' (great and high-soaring thoughts and perceptions) 'are gathered together.' 'Blessed is he that explains me', are the words put by the Church into the mouth of the Blessed Virgin, who is the Body of God.

XXIII

'Hoc est corpus meum; hic est enim calyx sanguinis mei, mysterium fidei.' 'Corpus Domini custodiat animam tuam in vitam aeternam.' It is not the Spirit, but the Body of God, God received by and beautifying the senses and the affections, by which we are saved. The spirit of God comes and goes; may be given and for ever withdrawn; but the Body and the Blood are the 'sure mercies of David', after having once tasted which the soul cries, 'How lovely are Thy tabernacles, O Lord of Hosts! My heart and my flesh have rejoiced in the living God'. 'Great', says St. Paul, 'is the mystery of righteousness', the righteousness of love; but not greater than the sacramental mysteries and initiations of that simply human love which is the highest order of nature.

XXIV

Perfect, easy, and abiding control over the senses is the fundamental condition of perceptive knowledge of God, and this control consists, not in the destruction of the senses and in the denial of their testimonies, but in the conversion of them from smoky torches into electric lights. 'He who leaves all for my sake shall receive a hundredfold *in this life*' of the same felicities—which we can only obtain by abandoning the pursuit of them.

XXV

The Author of the *Analogy*, the most prudent of theologians, considered that the seeds of vast developments of Christianity might still lurk unremarked in the words of Scripture; and there is nothing against good sense in supposing that some such developments may possibly be near and sudden. The certain corollaries of doctrine are, in some cases, as I have said, of far more import than the doctrine itself, without these inferences. Indeed, the infinite power of the doctrine of the Incarnation lies wholly in its corollaries. 'Where the *Body* is there the Eagles' (great and influential thoughts) 'are gathered together.' The 'Wisdom of the Ancients', as hidden in their mythologies, is mainly a meditation of that doctrine—which was the obscure instinct of all mankind, before Christ '*brought life and immortality to light*'.

XXVI

The Tree of Life and the Tree of Knowledge are the same. God prohibited and still prohibits to man the fruit of the Tree of Knowledge—the *summum bonum*—in order that it might and may be made the sweeter and truly sweet by delay and the merit of obedience. Man preferred and prefers to pluck the fruit before it thus ripened. The sensitive nature, or Eve, grasps at the ultimate and sensible good, before it has been made celestial, as all sensible good is, by self-denial. And years of sorrow, and such heroic sacrifice as few will submit to, are the conditions of God's consent to even the least degree of recovery of the lost treasure, in this life at least. But there are some who, even in this life, can say, 'Under the Tree where my Mother was debauched Thou has redeemed me'.

XXVII

Spirit craves conjunction with and eternal captivity to that which is not spirit; and the higher the spirit the greater the craving. God desires depths of humiliation and contrast of which man has no idea; so that the stony callousness and ignorance which we bemoan in ourselves may not impossibly be an additional cause in Him of desire for us. 'We are God's beasts', says St. Augustine. This, like all else that we can know of God, we know because it is faintly written in our own hearts. Theology teaches that all things subsist by junction with God—in man it becomes, if he will so have it *con*junction. Who knows but that a fatal junction with the dead rock may be a necessity of His infinite Spirituality, and an element of His infinite felicity? Human love requires to be grounded in the sensitive nature, in order to give counter-poise and reality to its spiritual heights. What if the love of God demands even a deeper foundation in the *un*spiritual, and in the junction and reconcilement of 'the Highest with the lowest'? There are obscure longings in the natural Man, glimpses of felicities of an 'Unknown Eros', which it is perhaps worse than vain to endeavour to indulge; a desire for fruits of the Tree of Knowledge which seem to promise that we 'shall be as Gods' if we partake of them. Maybe, to such of us as become Gods by participation, these fruits will be found fruits of the Tree of Life, as are other fruits, which, in the eating, have only a 'savour of death unto death', until they have been refused, in obedience to a temporary prohibition, and only tasted in God's season and with the divine appetite of grace. Meantime it is permitted, to such as have qualified themselves for such contemplations, to meditate upon the dim glimpses we can catch of such things, as they exist in God, who, as St. Thomas Aquinas teaches, *knows* matter, as He knows all His Creation, with love and desire.

XXVIII

The glowing purities and splendours of the perfect soul are protected, in their growth, by the dark slough and scab of her dead impurities. 'Let me see my sins rather than Thy graces', was the prayer of a Saint who knew to what dangers she would be exposed by a premature sight of her own loveliness. The 'veil of Moab' is, however, sometimes withdrawn for a moment, lest the fact that she is now become a worthy object of God's complacency should be too incredible; and she is allowed to behold herself, as with actual bodily vision, already more beautiful than Aphrodite.

XXIX

'The fullness of the Godhead *manifested* bodily.'

'God *manifest* out of Sion.'

'God *manifest* in the reality of our flesh.'

'The *manifestation* of the Sons of God, to wit the redemption of the Body.'

God was *not* 'manifest' in Our Lord in the body of His infirmity. He made Himself 'a worm and no man', that man might be no worm but a god. 'Touch me not, for I am not yet ascended.' Nor can He touch us, until we have attained to the redemption and transfiguration of the senses by participation in His spiritual Body. Some, as we may clearly infer from Christ's promises, and the witness of the Saints, *do* attain to this 'resurrection with Christ', to this 'manifestation', even now; but they are not many who 'so behold His presence in righteousness' that they thus 'wake up after His likeness and are satisfied with it' in this world; and, if this reward could be so expressed as to be intelligible and credible to all, none would ever attain it; for the necessary purification by faith and trial would be no longer possible were faith thus superseded by sight; and love would be universally profaned by a knowledge of and an impatience to realise the 'love of complacency', before its conditions were fulfilled and its order of sequence established.

XXX

Joshua represents the power of God in the conquest and conversion of the natural man. All the 'nations' of the Wilderness fell, one by one, before his sword, but when he came to Jericho, the last of these nations, in the 'extreme West', he was commanded not to fight, but persistently to surround it with the blasts of his trumpets, till the walls fell of themselves. This, being interpreted, means that the flesh or senses, the last power which is converted to God, does not fall through fighting; but that when all the other faculties of Man have been brought into subjection, then the flesh is to be attacked by an incessant repetition of the blast of the amazing truth that God demands also the allegiance and praise of the Body, which, being outside the field of the 'spiritual combat', and incapable of combating or of being combated by the forces which have subdued all else in Man, can only be overcome by the proclamation of an immediate and greater sensible good than that which it is called upon to abandon. Persistent and incessant affirmation of this truth is the only way of rendering it credible to the senses that an immense increase of their *present* felicity is the reward of submission to spiritual order. All the habits and phenomena perhaps of a long life have helped to render this crowning truth unintelligible and incredible, and a corresponding length of insistence upon it is necessary in order to remove the obstacles in the way of its acceptance.

N.B.—The West in Scripture and all ancient mythologies symbolised the flesh, as the East the spirit. Hence 'The coming of the Lord is as the shining light, which shineth from the East unto the West', conversion beginning in the Spirit and ending in the flesh. The Blessed Virgin is called by the Church the 'Rose of Jericho', because she represents the flesh, and gave our Lord His Body. In the Greek mythology, again, the great mystery of Persephone's descent into Hades was transacted in 'the extreme West'. To the learned, scores of instances of this use of the words East and West will suggest themselves.

XXXI

The fulfilment of God's promises, even in this life, to those 'who so believe that there shall be fulfilment of the things which have been promised', are so beyond hope, and beyond and unlike all previous imagination of those promises, that they are more incredible than were the promises themselves; and the difficulty of faith is thenceforward that of believing our own eyes and senses, and of accepting the self-evident; Nature being so illuminated and transfigured and become so much more natural than she was before, that she is herself clothed with incredibility.

XXXII

The glorified body, which some, for instance St. Theresa,
have seen in this life, is the ten-stringed harp of David, each
of its members constituting a distinct note, corresponding to
one of the ten spheres; and its tones and combinations of
tones are

> Sweet as stops
> Of planetary music heard in trance,

In the brief, virginal vision of natural love this fact is sufficiently apparent to take away all excuse for irreverent regard
for the Soul's blissful and immortal companion the Body,
and to supply the most *sensible* motive for whatever self-
denial may be necessary to the attainment of that vision in
perpetuity.

XXXIII

'Your bodies are the Temple of God', and they who go out of their bodies, i.e. their higher senses and powers of real apprehension, to seek Him, burn their powder in a dish instead of a gun-barrel, and the result is much flame but little force.

XXXIV

The foul, puritanical leaven of the Reformation has infected the whole of Christianity, and it is now almost impossible to speak with any freedom and effect on the doctrine of the Incarnation without shocking the sensibilities of those who, like the angels who fell, insist on being purer than God, and refusing worship to 'the fullness of the Godhead manifested bodily'.

XXXV

The Soul is the express Image of God, and the Body of the Soul; thence, it, also, is an Image of God, and 'the human form divine' is no figure of speech. In the Incarnation the Body, furthermore, *is* God, so that St. Augustine dares to say 'the flesh of Christ is the Head of Man'.

MAGNA MORALIA

MAGNA MORALIA

I

To LIVE HOLILY AND TO believe nothing is the way of that 'broad Church' which leadeth to destruction; for really so to live is worse than to live in harmony with its no-belief; since the conjunction of good in externals with evil in internals is as destructive a profanation as that of the opposite kind of conjunction, a real faith and an evil life.

II

In vulgar minds the idea of passion is inseparable from that of disorder; in them the advances of love, or anger, or any other strong energy towards its end, is like the rush of a savage horde, with war-whoops, tom-toms, and confused tumult; and the great decorum of a passion, which keeps, and is immensely increased in force by, the discipline of God's order, looks to them like weakness and coldness. Hence the passions, which are the measure of man's capacity for virtues, are regarded by the pious vulgar as being of the nature of vice; and, indeed, in them they are so; for virtues are nothing but ordered passions, and vices nothing but passions in disorder.

III

Favours and honours, when they become exceedingly great, become very manifestly what they are, and are far less dangerous to humility than lesser graces. The Beggar Maid was not nearly so likely to be made proud by her marriage with King Cophetua as the highest of his Court-Ladies would have been. Hence the subtlest and most successful device of the enemy is to persuade the soul that she cannot *please* God, much less excite His desire for her, and to represent as extravagant figures of speech His assurances to the contrary, such as 'The King shall greatly desire thy beauty' (*Concupiscet Rex decorem tuum*), 'I have longed for her', etc. True, she knows that none but a Goddess can be the desire of a God, but she is taught daily by His withdrawals that the divine beauty in her which He loves is His own reflection, and that, without it, she is at best but a flower in the dark.

IV

'Merit', as the word is used in Scripture and by the Church, means rather *capacity* than *right.* Faith 'merits' because, without faith, there can obviously be no capacity. Christ took upon Himself the flesh and human nature of the Blessed Virgin, 'through whom we have *deserved*' (or been made able) 'to receive the Author of Life'. Emptiness of self is the supreme merit of the Soul because it is the first condition of her *capacity* for God. 'My Soul shall make her boast in the Lord: the humble shall hear thereof and be glad.' The Soul's boast and merit, as it were her vanity, is the God-seducing charm of her conscious nothingness. She becomes through her

> Mere emptiness of self, the female twin
> Of Fullness, sucking all God's glory in.

The secret of obtaining and maintaining this humility, which is capacity, is not to deny the graces you have received, but to consider and be thankful for them all. If a sudden splendour shines about you in the night, and you see your Soul 'in the light of God's countenance', as beautiful as a Goddess, never forget it, but remember that you are verily that Goddess for Him so long as you acknowledge yourself to be of yourself nothing but dust and ashes and a house of devils.

V

St. Augustine says of Our Lord: 'Joseph was not less the father because he knew not the Mother of our Lord; as though concupiscence and not conjugal affection constitutes the marriage-bond. . . . What others desire to fulfil in the flesh, he, in a more excellent way, fulfilled in the spirit. . . . Let us reckon, then, through Joseph. . . . The Holy Spirit, reposing in the justice of them both, gave to both a Son.' Every true Lover has perceived, at least in a few moments of his life, that the fullest fruition of love is without the loss of virginity. Lover and Mistress become sensibly one flesh in the instant that they confess to one another a full and mutual complacency of intellect, will, affection, and sense, with the promise of inviolable faith. *That* is the moment of fruition, and all that follows is, as St. Thomas Aquinas says, 'an accidental perfection of marriage'; for such consent breeds indefinite and abiding increase of life between the lovers; which life is none the less real and substantial because it does not manifest itself in a separated entity.

VI

If a man's ways and works are good and great, it is because the man himself is better and greater, and because he cannot help the light of his unique personality showing in them. The greatest skill in composition, the most perfect finish of manners will never equal in value the least touch of that true style or distinction which consists in the manifestation of such a personality. On the other hand, the traits by which individuality is expressed are ordinarily so delicate and intangible that, though it may exist in a high degree in the man himself, its light cannot appear in his works or ways, unless these are purged from all coarseness and eccentricity.

VII

The greatest of contemplatives can only 'see in part and know in part', and he is like a child who is learning to distinguish upon an instrument the first notes, which combined, shall make the harmonies of heaven. These notes, indeed, are in themselves

Sweet as stops
Of planetary music heard in trance,

and are far more than enough to satisfy his present capacity for felicity. He does not attempt to combine them; for if he does, he finds that he is like a child educing confusion by striking his ignorant palm, here and there, upon the scale, instead of touching, with careful finger, its separate tones; for some tones, though all are celestial, jar when joined without intervention of others, and suggest passing doubts and confusions of spirit as to their being really heavenly.

VIII

When God has arduously wrought the six degrees of the Soul's new creation, and she is pronounced '*very* good', He rests from His labour, and bids her also to rest in the Sabbath of contemplation of His love and of His beauty as mirrored in herself. She 'wakes up after His likeness and is satisfied with it'; and greater wonders are wrought in her in one minute of mutual felicity than would be worked by a day of martyrdom, or a year of heroic action.

IX

He who renounces goods, house, wife, etc., for God's sake shall receive a hundredfold in this life, with life everlasting. But he who, having obtained this hundredfold return of all his natural delights transfigured, renounces this also, and acknowledges no consolation but his share in the agony of the Cross, shall shine for ever in heaven as a sun among the stars. Yet even he cannot escape his temporal reward, but hyssop itself, in touching his lips, becomes honey.

> Thus irresistibly by Gods embraced
> Is she who boasts her more than mortal chaste.

X

'What *reward* shall I give unto the Lord for all He has done to me? I will take the cup of salvation and call upon His Name.' A Lover does not want presents and services from his Beloved, but only that she should accept *His* presents and services.

XI

In proportion as our obedience—having been made perfect in obvious things—becomes minute and delicate, it becomes more meritorious and greatly rewarded. The difference between a commonly well-behaved woman and a high-bred lady consists in very small things—but what a difference it is!

XII

When the Tempter can no longer persuade us to our destructions by representing unclean things as clean, he perpetually harasses us, and endeavours to delay our progress by representing clean things as unclean. In the first stage of our advance we are purified by self-denial, in the second by denial, almost equally laborious, of the enemy's false charges.

XIII

Perception is hindered by nothing so much as by impatience and anxiety to attain it, and by trying to recall and dwell upon it when attained, 'If the Lord tarry, wait for Him', and then 'He will not tarry, but will come quickly'. To them that wait in quietness, attention, and silence of their own thought, all things reveal themselves, but

> None e'er hears twice the same who hears
> The songs of Heaven's unanimous spheres,

and, if you would receive new perception, you must, as St. John of the Cross says, 'Go forth into regions where nothing is perceived', and seek always, with David, to sing 'a *new* song'. These perceptions are 'treasures laid up in heaven'. We need not be anxious about them. 'The *heart* will not forget the things the eyes have seen.' There was a truly divine epicureanism hidden in the reply of the Greek philosopher to someone who wondered how it was that he seemed to despise the delight of love: 'I have tasted that sweetness once.' He that would be worthy of the Beatific Vision must fix his thoughts, not on the beatitude, but on the Vision. 'The Vision', writes St. Thomas Aquinas, 'is a virtue, the beatitude an accident'; and the Psalmist says: 'So let me behold Thy Presence in *righteousness* that I may wake up after Thy likeness and be satisfied with it.'

XIV

There is nothing outwardly to distinguish a 'Saint' from common persons. A Bishop or an eminent Dissenter will, as a rule, be remarkable for his decorum or his obstreperous indecorum, and for some little insignia of piety, such as the display of a mild desire to promote the good of your soul, or an abstinence from wine and tobacco, jesting, and small-talk; but the Saint has no 'fads', and you may live in the same house with him, and never find out that he is not a sinner like yourself, unless you rely on negative proofs, or obtrude lax ideas upon him, and so provoke him to silence. He may impress you, indeed, by his harmlessness and imperturbable good temper, and probably by some lack of appreciation of modern humour, and ignorance of some things which men are expected to know, and by never seeming to have much use for his time when it can be of any service to you; but, on the whole, he will give you an agreeable impression of general inferiority to yourself. You must not, however, presume upon this inferiority so far as to offer him any affront; for he will be sure to answer you with some quiet and unexpected remark, showing a presence of mind—arising, I suppose, from the presence of God—which will make you feel that you have struck rock and only shaken your own shoulder. If you compel him to speak about religion, he will probably surprise and scandalise you by the childishness and narrowness of his thoughts. He will most likely dwell with reiteration on commonplaces with which you were perfectly well acquainted before you were twelve years old; but you must make allowance for him, and remember that the knowledge which is to you a superficies is to him a solid. If you talk to *him* on such matters, he will kindly approve your pious expressions, and you will conclude that you had better drop the subject, for you will not find that he has that ardent interest in your spiritual affairs which you thought you had a right to expect, and which you have perhaps experienced from persons of far inferior reputation for sanctity. I have known two or three such persons, and I declare that, but for the peculiar line of psychological research to which I am addicted, and hints from others in some degree akin to these men, I should never have guessed that they were any wiser or better than myself or any other ordinary man of the world with a prudent regard for the common proprieties. I once asked a person, more learned than I am in such matters, to tell me what was the real difference. The reply was that the Saint does everything that any other decent person does, only somewhat better and with a totally different motive.

XV

The Masters of contemplation teach that its most perfect form is without exercise of thought or imagery; and that it consists in simple and perceived contact of the substance of the Soul with that of the Divine. Though this supernatural state has its analogue in Nature, in which touch sometimes supersedes all other communion, it is the last thing that mere Nature can conceive to be possible, much less attain to; and it has been further discredited by a certain appearance of stupidity which great contemplatives have shown in worldly matters. Indeed the habit of pure contemplation, though it is the very highest exercise of being, really induces a sort of stupidity, the Soul that practises it changing more and more from the form and life of the worm, which feeds and shifts from one leaf to another, and sees the little way it needs to see, in order to find its sustenance, to the form and life of the blind and motionless chrysalid, in which the substance of the worm becomes at first the pulp and material and merely potential life of an as yet inarticulate and unorganised being. When the worm is wholly thus transformed, the new nonentity—for God is henceforward its entity—begins, indeed, to acquire a prophetic soul, dreaming of things to come. It rather *is* than *has* faith; for it *is* 'the substance of things hoped for, the being evident of things unseen'; and, as the germ of divine life, which is buried in it, absorbs and organises more and more of its matter, the dreams become more and more like possible realities, and the dreaming soul, which had 'no bonds in its death' when it was a worm, begins to find its amorphous life and close imprisonment in the foul seat of its dead impurities more and more terrible, and only tolerable because it discerns that this conscious death and imprisonment is the necessary cathartic and purgative process by which the still remaining dross of the dead worm is gradually extruded into the slough which it longs to cast, in order that it may spread 'silver wings and feathers like gold' in a heaven of sunshine, liberty, perfume, honey and love.

XVI

All men in whom there is wisdom hate work. To be is better than to do, and in doing being is lost. St. Bernard sighs over having to leave the kisses of Truth, imparted only in leisure, for any other service of God, even that of preparing his novices for the like felicity; Lacordaire complains that, no sooner had he attained to the love of God, than all active service of God became hard and bitter to him; St. Francis of Sales declares that the Soul which is pure dishonours herself by doing, and thereby deprives God of that which alone He desires of her, her company and her person in contemplation. Of all work, thinking is most adverse to that tender and reverent listening at the feet of Wisdom, which is the true and acceptable idleness. But let not the idleness of the Spouse of God make slaves presume that they need not work.

XVII

Someone has said, 'Great is his happiness and safety who has beaten all his enemies, but far greater his to whom they have become friends and allies'. Happy he who has conquered his passions, but far happier he whose servants and friends they have become. The reconciled passions are the '*sure* mercies of David'.

XVIII

For the encouragement of the heart in the spiritual combat remember that no struggle, however faint or brief, is really unsuccessful. If we do not gain the victory, we at least diminish the future pain of defeat. Remember, also, that to rise and go on fighting after repeated disgrace and failure *is* victory over all three enemies of the soul, Sloth, Pride and Despair.

XIX

'There is no such malodorous corruption as that of rotten lilies'; no such Atheism and sin without hope of pardon as the Holy of Holies seen and known by the very senses, and yet denied and blasphemed; no gloomier foreshadowing of fate than the frantic misery of those who, having beheld the supreme flower of Love, long for ever for its profaned felicities, even while they are trampling it into dung, and mocking with idiot laughter its divinity.

XX

The occasional exaltation of the faculty of intellectual perception to heights far above the present ability of the moral
nature to follow is a fact of every man's experience. In the
mass of mankind these states of perceptive exaltation are
extremely rare. The visits of the Angels to them are few and
far between; but they are always frequent and bright enough
to fix themselves for ever in the memory, and to take away
all excuse on the plea of ignorance, for not striving for true
life; and their more frequent occurrence would constitute an
immense peril, as we see in the examples of many of those
persons who are called 'men of genius'. These enjoy more or
less habitually some measure of the vision which is accorded
to the rest of mankind only in far-separated moments. As a
rule, 'men of genius' are the worse and not the better for
this strange prerogative. They not only *mentally assent* to
Truth in doing falsely—which is a sin easily pardonable on
repentance—but they join evil with a present and *perceptive
knowledge* of good which is the sin against the Holy Ghost;
nay, they often feed the swine of their lusts with the pearls of
their perception; they look on the bared splendours of Purity
with eyes of the untransfigured passions; and their reward is
to be devoured by these as by dogs, instead of obtaining the
felicity of Endymion. God 'rains flesh' (good sensitively
perceived upon them) 'as thick as dust, and feathered fowls'

(real apprehensions) 'like as the sand of the sea', but while the manna and fat quails are in their mouths, He 'sends leanness into their souls'. 'Obey, therefore, thy holy Angel, for God is in him and He will not pardon.'

XXI

Sit, with Mary, at the feet of Christ, listening to His words, and be not busied with much serving. His words are real apprehensions, eternal states, which you make yours by consciousness and consent. Do not try to reconcile these apprehended realities. The prayer of the Prophet to be enabled to 'lie down with Him altogether' cannot be fulfilled *sensibly* or intelligibly in this life, though it is potentially realised when the will becomes wholly His. Leave the *form* of the future wholly to Him; not in anything insisting on your natural desires, which, if you attain to life, will all, indeed, be fulfilled beyond desire, though perhaps in modes the very reverse of those you expect and desire now. You do not truly 'love God and keep His commandments' by insisting, in desire, upon anything, even the salvation of your dearest and nearest. If you believe in and love God, you will effectually believe that He loves all who are capable of His love far better than you do, and you will be heartily sure that you will give, when you know all, a joyful consent to decrees which may seem to you now most hard and terrible.

XXII

God is the only reality, and we are real only so far as we are in His order, and He is in us. Hell, or Hades, was truly regarded by the ancients as the realm of shades, or phantoms and frightful dreams. We may know this by considering what phantoms, terrified by other phantoms, even the best of us are, in those seasons in which God withdraws His sensible presence and courage from our hearts, and we are frightened out of our wits by shadowy evils which our reason tells us are no evils; when some small prospective loss looks like ruin, some really trifling possible trouble keeps us awake all night with fear, and some little difficulty, which lifting a hand might remove, seems insuperable. All evils are phantoms, even physical pain, which a perfectly courageous heart converts, by simply confronting it, into present and sensible joy of purgation and victory. 'Savages' will laugh and sing under excruciating tortures, and many a Saint has been forbidden by his director to inflict on himself corporeal pain, because it had become a luxury.

XXIII

Who knows but that the greatest Cross in life, the knowledge that the only Dear One is for another's arms, may be changed, by fullness of sympathy, in fullness of fruition. 'His Law is exceeding broad', and let us not limit our eternal faculties by a temporal denial of their possibilities. In such case 'let our will have no word to say'. Let us be content with His promise that 'He will fulfil all our desires', we know not how.

XXIV

Ninety-nine men in a hundred are natural men, that is, beasts of prey; and it is mere insanity, in business matters, to deal with a stranger upon any other assumption than that he is a natural man, though we should veil our knowledge of the actual fact by a courteous recognition in words and manners of his better possibilities. No one ought to be disappointed or angry at finding a man to be what good sense was bound to expect him to be. We should rather wonder and give great thanks to God whenever we come across His greatest miracle, a supernatural, or honest and just man.

XXV

God is so infatuated with the beauty of the Soul to which
He is united that she cannot move a step, or speak a word *in
His presence*, without giving Him a new felicity. But His
presence is in her consciousness of it, and her grace thence
derived. For what woman's least action, look, or word is not
exalted into grace by her knowledge that the sight of her is
giving her Lover felicity? This consciousness is the 'easy yoke'
and the 'light burden' of which none but the perfect know
anything.

XXVI

The true Temple has veil within veil, and one is rent for the ingress of God every time the Soul dies upon the Cross, that is, resists interior temptations even to despair. 'Precious in the sight of the Lord is the death of His Saints'; and every Soul which is destined for Sanctity dies many times in this terrible initiative caress of God.

XXVII

God is not like Man, that great things should make Him
incapable of small ones. On the contrary, He has a micro-
scopic perception of the minutest additions to His 'glory', or
felicity of reciprocated Love; and to Him the least of these
additions is priceless.

XXVIII

Christ is the 'desire of all Nations'. Whatever good of the intellect, affections, or perceptions we have ever felt or can imagine is contained in the fruition of God. It will be as if all the infinite forms which lie hidden and possible to the sculptor in a block of marble should exist and be distinctly discerned at one and the same moment. Hence it is that, in the process of sanctification, each Soul is safely led by her own desires, which God gives her back glorified directly she has made a sincere sacrifice of them; and He says, not only 'Let the Heavens rejoice', but, 'Philistia be glad of me'.

XXIX

The baptism of water is initiation into Truth. It is therefore given to infants, since security is at the time taken that Truth shall be adequately presented. The baptism of fire is initiation into love, through a supernatural gift of perception of its beatitude.

XXX

In the earlier half of the Soul's progress, human loves are the interpretation and motive of the divine; but, in the second, the divine love becomes the interpretation and motive of the human. *Example:* the Holy Eucharist, in the beginning, is desired because it resembles the lower but still 'great' sacrament of human affection; afterwards the lower sacrament is explained and glorified by its resemblance to the higher. The latter, if you will consider it, is only a mystery; the former is not only a mystery but also, when regarded by itself, the greatest of anomalies.

XXXI

Many a man, who is pure and blameless in his own eyes and in those of the world, is, in God's sight, as foul as the piebald hair of leprosy; and many another, the shame and scandal of himself and his neighbours, on account of falls like those of David, is, through his ardour to cast the scab of his corruption, a man after God's own heart, which only sees the end.

XXXII

The world is not scandalised by anything so much as by the inconsistencies of believers, which it attributes to hypocrisy. But a great deal of 'inconsistency' and shortcoming is consistent with an entire absence of hypocrisy. The world having to do only with objects of the senses, discerns and believes a thing fully or not at all, and acts accordingly; and expects that Christians should do the same. But God and the truths of faith are 'infinitely visible and infinitely credible'; and discernment and belief vary infinitely in degree, from the obscure longing which cries, 'O God, if Thou be a God, save my Soul, if I have a Soul', to that of the Saint who sees God, as it were, face to face; and as faith thus varies, so varies the life which comes of it.

XXXIII

On one side of a gate in Athens the passenger was bid, by an inscription, to remember that he was but a man, and, on the other, that he was a god. 'Scire teipsum!' Otherwise though 'I have said, ye are Gods, ye shall all die like men'.

XXXIV

In all matters but the very few defined by the Church, Catholic opinion is liable to great though slow change, and it shares in or even leads the advances of civilisation, especially in its increasing mildness. For instance, an eternity necessarily intolerable for all persons out of the pale of the visible Church, is an opinion which is probably now only taught by the priests of Ireland and by Irish priests in England; and that only by way of alleviating their feelings towards the governing country.

XXXV

He who does the will of God is Christ's 'Mother, Sister, Brother', and all other relations, Son, Daughter, Bride, and Bridegroom; for 'Christ' says St. Augustine, 'is also the Bride, for He is the Body'. He could not be the 'satisfaction of all our desires', as He has promised to be, were it otherwise. Those who indeed know Him, possess the 'wishing rod', whereby they have only to desire any good, and to take the appropriate aspect of thought towards it, and it is at once obtained. 'The great serpent, Leviathan, King of Egypt' (Prince of sensible goods), 'became King of Israel'—the Proteus, also called 'Cetes, King of Egypt', by the Greeks and described by Homer as:

> Water, fire divine
> And every living thing that is;

the supreme desire, even while they know it not of all men, no longer takes every form by turn in order to elude capture, but does so in order to gratify every longing. He that hath ears let him hear.

XXXVI

'Happy is he who understands the mystery of Persephone. Over such an one Hades has no power.' He who has descended, with *Christ,* into hell, discerns the riches of the realm of Pluto for what they are—not *absolute* evils, but perversions and inversions of goods; 'Spirits in prison', purities cased, like chrysalids, in scales of corruption, but capable of cleansing and restoration to their original nature; and, when so restored, mightily helpful to the Soul which, retaining in her highest sanctification, and even in heaven, her natural character, cannot live her full life without natural delights.

Good people, who do not know that all evils are corrupted goods, in their anxiety to avoid evil, are apt to call the greatest goods, of which the worst evils are corruption, evil; and such may have to live maimed lives even in eternity; for all *denial* here is corresponding privation hereafter. This is our seed-time, and, in our harvest, we shall reap, in fruition, only what we have sown in confession. Simple *ignorance,* however, may co-exist with implicit acknowledgment.

XXXVII

The Visible Church is like the larva of the caddis-fly, from which the winged truth shall finally emerge, perfect and beautiful, but which at present inhabits a house of singular grotesqueness. Sticks, straws, stones, and shells in amorphous agglutination, giving much occasion for wonder and scandal to the Gentiles, and often causing anxiety to its inhabitant, who is apt to confuse these strange externals with its own life, and to think that attacked when these are criticised.

Have you ever, when riding, near sunset, or soon after sunrise, noticed the shadow of yourself and your horse on the road before you? Such a ridiculous shadow is the visible Church of the invisible.

XXXVIII

'My soul hath rejoiced in God my Saviour because He has regarded the lowliness of His handmaiden.' All joy is in the conjunction of opposites, height with depth, spirit with sense, honour with humility, above all, the Infinite with the finite. Hence an appearance of infatuation in all love. The highest Angel prostrates himself before a village maiden. She says, 'Behold the bondmaid of the Lord', to him who asks her to be His Bride and Mother. God lies swathed and swaddled in her flesh, 'reconciling the highest with the lowest'. Only lovers can think of these things; and they can think of nothing else.

XXXIX

The Soul before the Judgment-Seat of Hell. 'Answerest thou nothing? Hearest thou what great things they charge against thee: That thou madly sayest thou art the Spouse of God; that He is joined to thee in thy body; and that thou bearest offspring in His likeness?' But she said never a word. Her Divinity so hid Himself that, but for her adamantine faith she would have taken part with her accusers against herself.

XL

None, in this life at least, can taste the same spiritual sweetness more than once; and to those who practise the divine chastity of not seeking or desiring that it should be otherwise, God gives new and immortal delights every day.

'Who has ever multiplied his delights? or who has ever gained the granting of the most foolish of his wishes—the prayer for reiteration? It is a curious slight to generous Fate that man should, like a child, ask for one thing many times. Her answer is a resembling but new and single gift; until the day when she shall make the one tremendous difference among her gifts—and make it perhaps in secret—by naming one of them the ultimate.'—*Alice Meynell.*

XLI

The imagination has a mighty and most real and necessary function in the life of faith. 'We are saved by hope', but we cannot hope for what we cannot or do not apprehend. It is written, 'He shall fulfil all your desires', and 'your heart' (i.e. your desire) 'shall live for ever'. Every felicity, however dimly divined by the imagination as to its form, shall be fulfilled beyond thought and in a form more perfect than we know how to picture to ourselves, where, for them that believe, good things are laid up, 'beyond all that they know how to desire or imagine'. We *cannot* desire any good which is not a reality and a destined part of our eternity if we attain, and our imaginations of felicity are both samples and promises. The great praise of a contemplative life is that it is the seed-time of the celestial harvest. A true contemplative will receive into his heart and apprehension in half an hour more of these inspired initiatory pledges, which are seeds as well as promises, than another will acquire in a whole life-time; and the harvest will be in proportion to the sowing. The more extravagant and audacious your demands the more pleasing to God will be your prayer; for His joy is in giving; but He cannot give that for which you have not acquired a capacity; and desire is capacity. Take care, however, that you do not waste your strength and craze your brain by striving to acquire desires which are not human and natural; for heaven is but nature and humanity fulfilled, and God speaks His promises not in the active effort but the receptive silence of thought and endeavour.

XLII

Toleration, as it is now widely preached, may be a very one-sided bargain. It will not do to let falsehood and moral idiocy say to truth and honesty, 'I will tolerate you, if you will tolerate me'. There are truths which to many are incapable of proof, yet their denial is not to be tolerated, as the most tolerant society finds out when it is compelled to face the practical results of such denial. There are *not* 'two sides to every question', nor, indeed, to any. Nor can you convert men to truth by seeming to meet them half-way. The most powerful solvent is the sharpest opposite. You can best move this world by standing and making it clear that you stand upon another.

XLIII

Theologians teach that our ultimate felicity will consist in
the development of a single divine humanity made up of
innumerable unique and sympathetic individualities or
'members', each one shining with its proper and peculiar
lustre, which shall be as unlike any other lustre as that of a
sapphire is from that of a ruby or an emerald; and they
further teach that the end of this life is the awakening and
growth of such individualities through a faithful following of
the peculiar good which is each individual's 'ruling love';
since each has his ruling love, if he knew it, that is, his
peculiar and partial way of discerning and desiring the
absolute good, which no created being is capable of discerning
and desiring in its fullness and universality. Every man who
is humanly alive—and it must be admitted that there are a
good many to whom such life can only be attributed by a
charitable surmisal—is conscious that the bond of man with
man consists, not in similarity, but in dissimilarity; the happiness of love, in which alone is happiness, residing, as again
the theologians say, not in union but conjunction, which can
only be between spiritual dissimilars. That man is created in
the capacity for uniqueness of character is shown by the
human face, which is never at all alike in any two persons,
and of which the peculiarity is nothing but an expression of
the latent inherent difference which it is the proper work of
life to bring into actuality.

XLIV

Profanation is the conjunction of evil with good in the will, and if the evil were to be enlightened as to the felicities promised to those who 'seek first the Kingdom of God and His Righteousness', they would immediately profane those goods by desiring them primarily; and they would incur an eternal curse, like that of Tantalus, for having looked with desire on beatitudes which can only be enjoyed by those who have previously identified themselves, as it were, with Zeus, by absolute self-identification with his will.

XLV

'God leads us by our own desires', after we have once offered the sacrifice of them with full sincerity. The 'ruling love', the best-beloved good, which we offer to slay, as Abraham did Isaac, that very good is given back to us glorified and made indeed the thing which we desired. We have, with the 'Wise Man', to leave our own people and our father's house, before we can see 'Jesus with His Mother', but, after that, God bids us 'go back *another way, into our own country*'.

XLVI

If the central cores of light, beauty, love, reason, power, and order could—as perhaps they can—be presented in form to the human faculties, man would discern in them mere blackness, monstrosity, fatuity, weakness, terror, and chaos. The hideousness of some of the images worshipped by those among the ancients who best understood the Gods was not without its meaning.

XLVII

No created thing can be united with God, but all things owe their existence to junction with Him. Man is differentiated absolutely from the inferior creation by a capacity of *conscious* junction with Him which is *con*junction. 'All creatures', says St. Ignatius, 'are for man, and man for God.'

XLVIII

The 'reconcilement of the highest with the lowest', though an infinite felicity, is an infinite sacrifice. Hence the mysterious and apparently unreasonable pathos in the highest and most perfect satisfactions of love. The Bride is always 'Amoris Victima'. The real and innermost sacrifice of the Cross was the consummation of the descent of Divinity into the flesh and its identification therewith; and the sigh which all creation heaved in that moment has its echo in that of mortal love in the like descent. That sigh is the inmost heart of all music.

XLIX

The Catholic Church itself has been nearly killed by the infection of the puritanism of the Reformation. That human love which is the precursor and explanation of and initiation into the divine, that purity of purities which rebukes the purest by the revelation of their own unworthiness and incapacity, has been so deeply branded with the charge of impurity which its celestial candour rebukes in its mortal subjects, that modern preachers and pietists have studiously ignored or positively condemned as carnal and damnable the greatest of all graces and means of grace. 'The song of the Bride and the Bridegroom' is no more 'heard in the streets' of Jerusalem; these builders have refused the stone which Prophets, Apostles, and Saints regarded as the Head of the corner; and the doctrine of the Incarnation has been emasculated and deprived of its inmost significance and power. But the greatest darkness comes before the dawn, and the 'one mortal thing of worth immortal' is about to be enthroned in Catholic psychology as it never was before; for mortal love has retained and cultivated the sanctification which religion conferred upon it of old, though religion seems in great part to have forgotten having conferred it.

APHORISMS AND EXTRACTS

APHORISMS AND EXTRACTS

(Although Coventry Patmore did not include the following aphorisms and extracts in his original edition of *The Rod, The Root, and The Flower* they were included in the second edition as being similar in thought and form. These writings were found amongst his papers after his death under the headings, *Unpublished Lines, Jottings For Poems,* and *Thoughts For Poetry And Meditation.* In re-printing them, I have included some hitherto unpublished fragments from the manuscript of *The Rod, The Root, and The Flower* now in the Nottingham University Library.—Editor's Note.)

O World
Rebuked by utter silence of its best.

The modern wise,
That, like the men of Sodom, cannot see
The gate before their eyes.

The Daisy Innocence,
That gazes unconfounded on the Sun.

What is a woman without tears?

Save by the Old Road none attain the new,
And from the Ancient Hills alone we catch the view.

[*Pain in all love.*]
From the small life that loves with tooth and nail
To the thorn'd brow that makes the heavens pale.

Compare the sudden change in the religious life at maturity
to the sudden autumnal infusion of sweet juices into the sour
and bitter fruit of summer.

Let the response of her delight
Be tender, timely, slight.

Ah, great, sweet Lord, make Thou of little me
Only a soft reciprocal of Thee.

When the soul owns herself sincerely to be nought
The whole of heaven flows in as freely as a thought.

Who speaks the things that Love him shows
Shall say things deeper than he knows.

Pride gives no food unless he can a feast:
The quality of grace is goodness in the least.

A song
Loud with the truth which cannot be expressed.

List the forgotten spheres,
Till, like a lute-string that a trumpet hears,
Thy answering soul will magic airs resound.

[*Heaven*]
Softness, sweetness, ineffable variety and mutability,
Perception of each other's inmost bliss,
And no desire or any thought for anything but this.

To lie within His heart without annoy,
   And only by believing,
   And only by receiving,
Sans question of desert or scruple coy,
   To give bliss to the Giver—
   O bright, full-flooded river
Of nameless and intelligible joy!

With vision of Thee do Thou my heart so feed
That every word I breathe shall be a deed.

Faith is the light of the flame of love.

May I love Him with love and joy like them
So virginal, so wifely, so motherly, so marvellous!

Potency of Joy
To do, resist, or to destroy.

Men oft see God,
But never know 'tis He till He has passed.

I am
As one that knows a tune but cannot sing.

'I will lay me altogether down in peace', (*Ps. lv.* 8)
Till my posture is a Sacrament.

With Thee,
A Goddess made of amethystine light:
Without thee, the most rank
And filthiest clot of carrion that ever stank.

Love that
Burns with desire of burning more and more.

God, in whose image we were made,
Let me not be afraid
To trace Thy likeness in what best we are.

All day for God to work or fight,
And be within His arms all night.

A million crowned Brides, and every queen
As diverse from the rest as red from green.

From me, thine altar, let no strange fire hiss.

Ah, heavenly fame,
Aye to do good and be for aye unknown.

Until at last
The bush of knowledge blazes with God's love.
Thou hidst Thyself from me
Who have lost all and even myself for Thee.

I will not go beyond my door
To hunt for poor.
I am the poorest person that I know
That I should meet, where'er I go.

The eye of innocence renew'd in age.

All I ask for the reward of love
Is but to love thee more.

Shine, shine, and fill thy Flower
With colour, honey, and perfume.

Wandering with Thee alone among
The mountains of eternity.

Sin, by which Heaven obtained the exquisite edge of sorrow.

And others
Are blamed for faults they long since left behind.

The patient man, whate'er his hardship be,
Enjoys already sweet eternity.

Truth made good by life.

I have deserved hell, and my punishment is bliss.

Unelated, undejected, centred in its own humility.

The simple and the pure, into whose hearts
Truth falls, like dew into a fleece of wool.

The honour of the world, that waits to crown by name,
I hate thrice worse than shame.

[*One Good better than Another.*]
The flame that shoots above the fire.

The soul
Sucking its life from the deep breasts of love.

Just war and wedlock, which make right
Nature's twain joys, to kiss and fight.

It doth come
Of being deaf that men are dumb.

Whence joy and sorrow, in divine embrace,
Look down, with pitying face,
Towards the poor, terrestrial peaks of bliss,
Where pain and pleasure kiss.

Better blood-letting War than the foul-blooded ease
That breeds such boils as these.

In the soft arms of happy certitude.

A bee upon a briar-rose hung
And wild with pleasure suck'd and kiss'd;
A flesh-fly near, with snout in dung,
Sneer'd 'What a Transcendentalist!'

'O loving hint answering my longing guess',
And whispering softly to my wildest wishes, 'yes'.

[*The People.*]
'Tis but a toss-up whether they cry
Hosanna, or Crucify!

The only kindness Wise can show to Fool
Is, firm to hold him on the whipping-stool.

Truth-teaching is a trait he only knows by half
Who does not o'er his labour sing and laugh.

As of old the truth,
Now falsehood has become self-evident.

Of God's love the many-coloured rays
Grow only visible in the incense of praise.

Love that weakens with its sweet the knee
That drops adoringly to thee.

Ah, Lord,
Thy vine still gives Thee vinegar to drink.

He found me in the desert, and then fell
In love with my exceeding loneliness.

A bee, beloved, is least of fowls with wings,
Yet is her fruit the sweetest of sweet things.

Who search for truth and do not start from God
For a long journey should be shod.

For the foul fume is matter of sweet flame.

Heaven, which is
The eternal agony of God's first kiss.

Not little children, but the man
That was as one of them, is he
Who Heaven's kingdom enter can
By right of his simplicity.

Science, the agile ape, may well
Up in his tree thus grin and grind his teeth
At us beneath,
The wearers of the bay and asphodel,
Laughing to be his butts,
And gathering up for use his ill-aim'd cocoa-nuts.

How should they win,
Who care not for the prize?

The darkness that precedes increase of light.

To evolve the sounds of joy and ruth
Out of pure law and hated truth.

The kiss of silence and of light.

This brightest hope is but thick smoke
By the sweet light in which the least saint lives.

As parched Egypt longs for rising Nile,
So I for thee.

Thy love is an incessant trouble in my breast, like one of
those little quiet wells where the upheaval of the sand never
ceases.

Like milk from the kind, impatient breast, so willing to
feed that, on the approach of the baby's mouth, it waits not
to be pressed.

As a fountain seeks in air the hidden level of its far-off
source.

Respiration and inspiration correspond to the life of faith.

I desire nothing now but to desire Thee more.

Redemption was but an incident of the Incarnation, which
did more for those who did not require it than for those who
did. It was *these* things—i.e. the relations of it to the Just,
especially to Blessed Virgin—which the angels desired to
look into.

[*Thought*]
Idiots that take the prologue for the piece,
And think that all is ended just when it begins.

I love Thy beauty Whom as yet I cannot see; and Thou lovest me, although as yet I do not exist.

Modern science goes towards the truth, as, when we walk towards the sinking sun, the world while we walk rolls the other way.

If a man thinks he knows anything as he ought, let him know that he knows nothing.

The body of the Lord. The beauty of this vesture is only seen on the wearer.

Give me to desire all which Thou desirest to give.

The unimaginable freedom, felicity, honour, and spirituality of heaven require unimaginable bonds, anguish, shame, and materiality, as their counterpoise and the conditions of their reality. In the crucified seraph, St. Francis saw the only recorded vision of the state of the Blessed in Christ.

Mother is more than and includes Bride.

The Holy Spouse of Christ, can she become the poor strumpet of the State?

Good people and religious are the first to say, 'He hath a devil' of anyone whose way is widely different from and maybe greatly higher than their own.

The Blessed Virgin is co-redemptrix with Christ. His visit converts the soul to acknowledge the truth and to obey it in intention, destroying the old Adam. Her visit converts the body, giving gentle disposition and affection, destroying the old Eve.

Chastity is so splendid a virtue that in praising it we do not oppose it to vice—whose name is unknown to it—but only to lesser degrees of itself; i.e. an ordinarily pure marriage.

God has declared to us His mystic rapture in His Marriage with Humanity in twice saying, 'Hic est Filius meus dilectus in quo bene complacui'. He expressly and repeatedly calls this marriage, and pronounces the marriage of Man and Woman to be its symbol. *This is the burning heart of the Universe.*

The love of Son for Mother and Mother for Son is more than the love of Bride and Bridegroom, and includes it.

[*Blessed Virgin*], God made thy womb the place of His delight, and said (ah, happy me!) that every *other* who did His will was even as thou His Mother.

'A woman heavy with child denotes the state in which the formation of good from truth is proceeding.' 'He who does my will (i.e. *forms* good by truth) is my Mother', etc.

The Word made flesh . . . 'I love *you*' made flesh of my flesh.

'The Virgin's womb.' The narrowness of that dwelling, the darkness, the mode of nourishment: He could not hear, nor see, nor taste, nor move; He lay at all times fixed and bound;

> And by that rapture of captivity
> He made us free
> His blissful prisoners likewise to be.

'The good of infancy is the habitation of the Lord with man', i.e. He is an *infant* in those who are His. 'He who believes is my Mother.'

There is a thing on which I dare not ponder, lest with Cain and Judas I despair.

Is this great Sodom, saved by its half-score of just whom it detests?

None can be eternally united who have not died for each other.

Making no vows, but obeying each new behest with a spirit of new love.

[*Eden.*] God in creation called all things one by one 'Very good', except Man and Woman, whose perfection was suspended till Gabriel said, 'Hail, Mary, full of Grace!' And God said, 'This is my beloved Son, in whom I am well pleased'.

'The primitive human form is not in the form of the body, but in a most perfect form known to the Lord alone, which conspires and tends to that . . . The human form is put on by all angels and men, but the Lord alone is man.'

How sweet a rainbow of hope arises when the cloud of compunction sheds its showers in the sunshine of grace.

'Every *affection* comprises things innumerable, for it involves within itself the whole life of a man from his very infancy.'

Truth, the air in which Love flies and sings.

Trees which have double blossoms bear no fruit.

The night-brawler, remembering how he once met God in a daisied field, may feel

'Some saving sorrow of offended love'.

Nothingness is capacity, and night the opportunity of light.

He wipes away her tears of repentance so gently that she sheds ten times more.

Our state still changing 'twixt too much love and none.

The more we live in communion the more individual shall God's kiss be.

Thus shalt thou grow:
By little and by little and most rapidly.

The dull and heavy hate of fools.

Thou'st turned my substance all to honeycomb,
Each atomy a cell of discrete sweet.

When Jesus came
The world was all at peace in utter wickedness.

Bound fast
In marriage strange whose honeymoon comes last.

He ruddy with her love,
She splendid with his light.

The song that *is* the thing it says.

In the eternal peace and tempest of delight.

It is not fit that men who hear these songs should not know
that I am no better than themselves. May I so do my works
that men seeing them may praise my Father, and leave me
from them.

Exempt,
In the safe shadow of the world's contempt.

The *same* press applied to the wheel of life causes it to go ever faster and faster. Dread greatly if to-day you love only as much as you did yesterday; for your fall has already begun.

The soul becomes nuptially united with God and impregnated by Him the instant she perfectly submits, and says, 'Behold the handmaid of the Lord: Be it done to me according to Thy word'.

Peter made those humble protestations of love and reparation for his three denials (Sea of Tiberias) and our Lord did not say, 'You have formerly denied me thrice, and are not worthy to feed my sheep', but, 'Feed my sheep'; for he loved much, having been pardoned much: for love is the Prophet's secret; and those who have best fed God's sheep are those who have learned much love through much pardon.

The hot desert and the putrid marsh—of modern thought and feeling.

The Son gave Himself for Man: the Father gave His Beloved for him.

The frontiers between sense and spirit are the Devil's hunting-grounds.

Love not only levels but subjects.

Man can never purify himself in the least degree except by arriving at the purity of Christ, which is impossible to the highest Angel.

May I know by love and speak by silence.

That which is unique in the soul is its true self, which is only expressed in life or art when the false self has been surrendered wholly. In saints this surrender is continual: in poets, etc., it is only in inspired moments.

Good and truth only differ as fire and flame.

None can move this world unless he stands upon another.

We must confess our sins in order to obtain pardon; but we must *see* our sins in order to confess. How few of those who think that they have confessed and been pardoned have ever seen their sins!

May all my words be like Thine, which have no outward comeliness or subtilty, but 'which enlighten understandings and inflame hearts, and excite to compunction and give manifold consolations'.

Rivers that give to Ocean but its own.

Dear Lord, for forty years I tried to raise in the wilderness a house for Thy abode. I painfully gathered bricks, and worked a bit of cornice here, and there a capital; but as I put it together all would suddenly fall, and still I gathered up material, though the more I gathered the greater seemed the chaos; but one day, why none could tell, except perhaps that I felt more despair than ever I had done before, I heard a winnowing of unseen wings, and lo, the bricks and stones all took their place,

> And a gay palace fine
> Beyond my deepest dreamt design,
> May He who built it all
> Take care it does not fall.

Saints like soldiers, who, to acquire booty, wish for war (persecution, temptation, etc.).

[*Divine Love.*] As when one dreams of what is at the moment a reality.

The pride of the soul that has God for her spouse should be greater than that of Lucifer.

Let me love Thee so that the honour, riches, and pleasures of the world may seem unworthy even of hatred—may be not even encumbrances.

The cloud that is light to Israel is blackness to Egypt.

I will keep my little house clean for thee; my bed shall be bright, and the sheets shall smell of lavender. Others come to their spouses loaded with acceptable wealth. Blessed are they. But I bring no dowry but a pleasant voice. And I am content if thou art.

As the Word of God is God's image, so the word of man is *his* image, and 'a man is known by his speech'.

By this you may know vision: that it is not what you expected, or even what you could have imagined, and that it is never repeated.

No love shall live for ever in the Beloved which is not heartily willing to die for ever for him.

Pardon is not over and done with once for all, but incessant contrition and incessant pardon are the peculiar dainties of those in heaven who have forfeited the dainties of first innocence.

My call is that I have seen the truth and can speak the living words which are born of having seen it.

When God stretches forth His rod over the Egypt of the heart, what we thought was dust we find is lice.

[*Draught of fishes.*] I thank Thee for refusing so long my prayer, for when Thou delayest a gift it is always to give it more abundantly.

Let me set about this despised work with long-animous charity and a joyful sense of the purity and privacy of my sole reward, Thy love.

Swedenborg, the Anti-Christ, whose doctrine would deceive the very elect, but for special grace of God, i.e. deceive them by giving the whole doctrine of the Church and denying the *life* of the Church, i.e. its authority.

The internal and external are perfectly distinct from each other; but where they are together the internal is in the external as in its adequate form, which form can only act from it as an effect from its cause. *The external lives from the internal, but it is only by the external that the internal can act* as a cause in this lower sphere, and produce effects there. 'For the man is not of the woman, but the woman of the man. For the man was not created for the woman, but the woman for the man.... But yet neither is the man without the woman, nor the woman without the man in the Lord. *For as the woman is of the man, so also is the man by the woman;* but all things of God.'

... The Son (Word) is the external of the Father, man the external of the Son, woman the external of man.

He is irrational, however well he may be able to reason, who does not clearly see that good is good, and truth truth.

Self-doubting hope, sufficient for sure peace.

The life of love includes all the requisite wisdom of that love. 'The wise are above books.'

'I have yet many things to say to you, but you cannot bear them now.' Not because they are so unlike your mortal experiences, but because they are so like.

Man against Hell, without the help of God, is as a rabbit against the Russian empire.

My net, at last, is full of fishes, but I cannot draw it to land without Thy help.

Long I mistook seeing the end for being in the way.

'Nothing is so easy to men of goodwill as goodwill itself, and this is all that God requires.' Every act of goodwill permanently and sensibly increases goodwill. Trifling acts of goodwill are often more efficacious in this way than great ones. A flower given in kindness and at the right time profits more, both to giver and receiver, than some vast material benefit in which the goodwill is hidden by the magnitude of the act. Some little, sensible, individual touch from the hand of Our Lord may convert the heart more than the contemplation of His death for us.

Unless the Lord had come into the world and united the human with the divine, the perceptive faculty of good and truth would have been utterly lost to man. It is to the existence of the few that constitute the *living* Church that is owing the existence of any perceptive faculty now.

How could I treat Thee as a Wife should her Husband: how kiss and laugh with Thee: how bear Thee in my bosom, if I saw the least ray of Thy sanctity, which would burn me up? In Thy unapproachable Saints I must view Thy Sanctity, where I can safely look on it, as on the Sun in water.

The soul cannot attain to enjoy God in this life, but she can attain to know that God is enjoying her; and this is the greatest joy of a true wife.

I have an alabaster box, sweet speech full of the praise of God, left to me from the riches I have left. I come, like that other sinner, to break it over Thee, and what this woman hath done shall be told in all the world, not to her honour, but to His, who by much pardon breeds exceeding love.

Holy indignation is a proof that we should do the same thing ourselves, and easy tears are a certain sign of a hard heart.

Do not violate the integrity of the unknown bliss by forms and apprehensions.

[*Finding in the Temple.*] The life of the soul on Earth is the alternate losing and finding of Jesus. It goes but two days' journey in its ordinary business and misses God. Has to return upon its path. Finds Him in the Temple, its own *body*.

O, Holy Mother, who wast not afraid to undertake to utter the Word, but simply answered to Gabriel's invitation, 'Behold the Handmaid of the Lord'; so I, invited by God to speak such a word as has not been uttered since thou inspiredst the Florentine, will not refuse the vocation of Him, Who has in this regarded the humility of my soul, His handmaid, who trusts to Him the whole execution of that which He has put upon her.

Nothing remains with man unless it is insinuated with some delight.

He who renounces goods, house, wife, etc., shall have a hundredfold in this life, with life eventually; and he who, having obtained this hundredfold, renounces this also, shall shine for ever as a sun among stars.

Moses, though excluded by his one sin from the Promised Land, was afterwards one of those on the Mount of Transfiguration.

Let dust keep down.

The enthusiasm for goodness which shows that it is not the habit of the mind.

Let peace be peace, war war.

We fly from the barbarian invasion, devastating our own country as we go, and cry, lo, they prophesied falsely who said the barbarians would destroy our land.

The God long wandering in search of some maiden whose chastity was so great that her body would offer no opposition to permeation by his.

The union perpetually increased by recurrent agonies of sacrifice on the maiden's part. Her fathomless virginity.

Enough's a surfeit to the soul.

My love not only dares the most searching light of philosophy, but requires it.

The utter forgetfulness of each generation as to the other's good.

And when I woke, it was as if a bird should wake and find a flood had risen in the night, and there was no world but water.

We are indeed already risen from the dead, but we are still bound with our grave-clothes.

Sins in the regenerate are only the breaking forth of leaves in the trunk that is felled.

Their death is Easter who make life their Lent.

The strong efforts of man are nothing but the crazy convulsions of extreme weakness.

Life's warp of Heaven and woof of Hell.

Give to my immortality nothing but immortal affections.

Liars though ye be, ye cannot make a thing not to be by saying that it is.

The mirth of the world is really the grin of despair.

The fine sheets of thin cloud before a storm shining with untransient lightning. Compare to corporeal joy of love in a *body* 'full of grace'.

Happy the Man who is his Mistress's first love: happy the woman who is her Lover's second.

Modern philosophers, that wisely keep to sandy shallows, like shrimps, for fear of bigger fish.

The mutations of things spiritual and celestial. Life without such changes would be uniform, consequently *nothing*; nor would goodness and truth be known or distinguished, much less perceived.

Man hates truth; and Our Lord conquered not through but in spite of being this Truth, in spite of Prophecies, Miracles, or Prodigies, which only made men hate and disbelieve Him more.

Secret saints, unstain'd with human honour.

Not only is song the bloom of Science, but the seed is always in the flower.

When Our Lord died, all Creation, which held its life from Him, necessarily felt the pangs of death also.

If you wish to be commonly good, the easiest, indeed the only way, is to be heroically so.

If the Son is the Bride of the Father and the Husband of the Church, it follows that the male soul may be the Bride of Christ and the Husband of the female.

In the Lord there was a union of the Human essence with the divine, but in the case of man with the Lord there is not union but conjunction.

The Lord has union with Jehovah; but man has not union with the Lord, but conjunction. . . . This reciprocal union is what the Lord means when He attributes to the Father what belongs to Himself.

The image of this reciprocal union is probably in the ideal, unfulfilled marriage of man and woman.

An idea of God formed from the human, whatsoever quality it be, providing only it flows from the good of innocence, is accepted.

[Communion of Saints.] . . . One life with a million mouths sucking the single honey of His love.

God usually answers our prayers so (much more) according to the measure of His own magnificence than of our asking, that we do not know His boons to be those for which we besought Him.

The proper study of mankind is woman.

All life and joy is motion. That of time and vulgar souls is linear, and so not without change of place; and good to them is known only in the coming and the going. With souls of grace it is not so. They go about a centre, which planetary motion is their joy. They have also a self-revolving motion, which is their peace. Their own regularity enables them to perceive the order of the universe. Their ears with inmost delectation catch the sound of the revolving spheres. They live in fruition of the eternal novelty.

The union a source of incessant active chastity.

[*The Four Steps.*] Faith in God the Father, the Son, the Holy Ghost, the Blessed Virgin.

May I so speak that the wise of this world, though they may understand nothing, may still say, 'The speaker of such words can scarcely be quite a fool'.

God advancing slyly step by step, till at last He lays hands upon His little bird.

For happy 'tis to live from care exempt
In the safe shadow of the world's contempt.

231

Blessed are they that have to bear (and can bear) the persecution of its praise.

He preserves interior silence best who talks most on indifferent things.

Light words are weighty sins.

Thou wilt not tarry if I wait for Thee.

The Devil pierces our thoughts with the needle of truth in order that he may draw after it the long thread of lies.

From stocks or stones *eliciting delight.*

The single apple which has by accident been left in the leafless orchard.

And Nature is another name for sin.

[*Virginity.*] He who bears the flag is most the soldier, though he does not fight. And he who nobly upholds the honour for which man is procreated helps as much as any the conservation of the race.

The following aphorisms were suppressed by Coventry Patmore in his original manuscript, now in the Library of Nottingham University, but are printed here as interesting examples of the poet's thoughts.

Hate pleasure, if only because it is the only way of obtaining it.

Those who ask for a sign shall have many.

The best way you can advance the world's good is to attend diligently and exclusively to your own.

'We should communicate, not only for our soul's benefit, but also to satisfy our Lord's exceeding longing for us.' *De Condron.*

Think often of Mary, that dear little child with child of God, if you be like Her.

Woe to him with whom the angels talk unless with them he dares to walk.

The Greeks were quite right in putting Socrates to death. Their myths contained a vast body of true and living doctrine for which Socrates offered to supply no substitute while destroying it.

Most of those who read this book will be the worse for it; for the light which does not purify blasts.

SELECTED BIBLIOGRAPHY

The Life and Times of Coventry Patmore, by Derek Patmore. Constable. 1949.

Coventry Patmore. Memoirs and Correspondence. (2 Vols.) by Basil Champneys. George Bell & Sons. 1900.

Coventry Patmore. Literary Lives Series, by Sir Edmund Gosse. Hodder & Stoughton. 1905.

Patmore. A Study In Poetry, by Frederick Page. Oxford University Press. 1933.

The Idea of Coventry Patmore, by Osbert Burdett. Humphrey Milford. 1921.

The Great Victorians. Essay on Coventry Patmore by Herbert Read. Nicholson & Watson. 1932.

Positions et Propositions, by Paul Claudel. Gallimard. 1934.

Poèmes de Coventry Patmore. Translations by Paul Claudel, with Introduction by Valery Larbaud. Nouvelle Revue Française. 1912.

A Selection of Poems by Coventry Patmore. Edited and Introduced by Derek Patmore. Grey Walls Press. 1948.

The Poems of Coventry Patmore. Edited with and Introduction by Frederick Page. Geoffrey Cumberlege. Oxford University Press. 1949.

CPSIA information can be obtained at www.ICGtesting.com
Printed in the USA
BVOW03s0434230913

331813BV00009B/138/P